Fun with Biblical Words

Fun with Biblical Words

More Than Sixty Greek and Hebrew Words
to Revolutionize Your Study of God's Word

Tom Hobson

WIPF & STOCK · Eugene, Oregon

FUN WITH BIBLICAL WORDS
More Than Sixty Greek and Hebrew Words to Revolutionize Your Study of God's Word

Copyright © 2024 Tom Hobson. All rights reserved. Except for brief quotations in critical publications or reviews, no part of this book may be reproduced in any manner without prior written permission from the publisher. Write: Permissions, Wipf and Stock Publishers, 199 W. 8th Ave., Suite 3, Eugene, OR 97401.

Wipf & Stock
An Imprint of Wipf and Stock Publishers
199 W. 8th Ave., Suite 3
Eugene, OR 97401

www.wipfandstock.com

PAPERBACK ISBN: 979-8-3852-2690-0
HARDCOVER ISBN: 979-8-3852-2691-7
EBOOK ISBN: 979-8-3852-2692-4

VERSION NUMBER 07/17/24

Biblical quotes, when they are not the author's own translation, follow the New Revised Standard Version Bible, copyright © 1989 by the Division of Christian Education of the National Council of the Churches of Christ in the U.S.A. Used by permission. All rights reserved. Often, the two translations closely coincide. Quotes that are uniquely NRSV or any other Bible translation are marked according.

Quotes from ancient authors use the Loeb Classical Library version when available, with adjustments in the translation where warranted in the eyes of the present author, except for the works of Philo and Josephus, where the author bases the quotes partly on the Greek and English editions found in BibleWorks. The quote from Clement of Alexandria in chapter 4 is from volume 23 of the *Fathers of the Church* series (see bibliography).

This book is greatly indebted to the loving companionship of my wife of forty-five years, Catherine. Her emotional support is what makes this book her contribution to the world of biblical scholarship as much as it is mine.

Contents

Abbreviations | x
Introduction | xi

1. Count It All Dung!—*skubalon* | 1
2. Iron Age Super Mom: The Woman of "Valor"—*ḥayil* | 4
3. How Did *Agapē* Become the Ultimate Word for Love?
   —*agapē, agapaō, ḥesed* | 7
4. What Does the Bible Teach about Obscene Language?
   —*aischrologia* | 10
5. What's Wrong with Getting Drunk, Paul?—*asōtia* | 14
6. Is Elohim Jehovah, or a Pantheon?—*elohīm* | 18
7. Creation and How It Happened—*baraʾ, min* | 22
8. Firmament: Dome or Atmosphere?—*raqiʿa* | 25
9. Sea Monsters in Genesis?—*tannīn* | 28
10. Managing God's Masterpiece—*kabash, radah* | 30
11. Adam's Mate: A Point-By-Point Counterpart—*negedō* | 33
12. Methuselah: Man of "Vitality"—*lēḥ* | 35
13. The Ancient Flat Earth: A Modern Lie—*eretz, tēbēl, oikoumenē* | 38
14. Messiah's Mother: Virgin or Young Woman?—*ʿalmah, betulah* | 41
15. No Room For the Inn—*katalyma* | 44
16. Brothers or Cousins of Jesus?—*aḥ, adelphos* | 47
17. Christ the Builder?—*tektōn* | 50

CONTENTS

18. Same-Sex Intimacy: What Does Jesus Say?—*aselgeia* | 53
19. Eunuchs in Biblical Times—*sarīs, eunuchos* | 56
20. Concubine Versus Married Woman in the Bible
    —*pilegesh, porneia* | 59
21. Desire, Lust, and Coveting: It's All the Same Word!
    —*epithymia, epithymeō* | 62
22. Belial and Sons—*beliyyaʿal* | 65
23. Killing, Smiting, and Other Casualties—*hikkah, ḥalal, harag, hēmīth, ratzaḥ* | 68
24. Laughing, Playing, and Beyond Child's Play—*tzaḥaq* | 71
25. Who Are You Calling Boy?—*naʿar, baḥur, ben, yeled* | 74
26. Does God Do "Bad"—*raʿ* | 77
27. Divine Necessity—*dei, proorizō* | 80
28. Draw Versus Drag: How Does God Bring People to Faith?
    —*helkō* | 83
29. What Was Wrong with Leah's Eyes?—*rak* | 86
30. Thief or Terrorist: What Kind of Criminal Was Crucified with Jesus?
    —*lēstēs, harpax, kleptēs* | 89
31. Holiness: Being Different From a Dysfunctional World
    —*hagios* | 92
32. Does God Repent? And How Should We?—*niḥam, metanoeō* | 96
33. Life on the Straight and Level—*yashar* | 100
34. What's the Difference between Spirit and Soul?
    —*ruaḥ, pneuma* | 102
35. Soul or Life? The Double Meaning of *Psychē*—*psychē, zōē, bios* | 105
36. *Koinōnia*: What We Share in Common—*koinōnia* | 108
37. Be Ye Perfect? Exactly What Does Jesus Mean?—*teleios* | 112
38. The Dark Side of the Word *Shalom*—*shalom* | 115
39. Lawlessness: What Happens When Law Itself Becomes Lawless?
    —*anomia* | 117
40. Stomping on the Powerless—*laḥatz, ʿashaq* | 120
41. Does God Care More about Justice Than about Sex?—*mishpaṭ* | 123
42. The Immigrant in the Hebrew Bible—*gēr* | 125

CONTENTS

43. How to Define Hate—*miseō* | 129
44. Favoritism: God Hates It—*prosōpolēmpsia* | 132
45. Comfort, Encourage, Exhort, or Beg?—*parakaleō* | 135
46. Worthy, Sizeable, or Sufficient?—*hikanos* | 138
47. Leave, Allow, or Forgive?—*aphiēmi* | 141
48. Authority: Power or Right to Act—*exousia* | 144
49. Sorcery, Or Use of Drugs?—*pharmakeia* | 148
50. R-Rated Prophets—*erastai, shiggēl* | 151
51. Russia and China: Major Players in the Last Days? —*Magōg, Rōsh, Sinim* | 154
52. A*nti* Ain't What We Thought It Was—*anti* | 158
53. God Is "Hyper" about Us—*hyper* | 161
54. The One and Only Melchizedek Priest—*aparabaton, taxis* | 165
55. Words Almost Never Heard in the Bible—depression, retirement, tolerance, fun, cat | 168
56. How to Do Word Studies for Yourself | 171

Bonus Chapter 1—Fun in the Septuagint | 174
Bonus Chapter 2—Fun in the Latin Bible | 178

Bibliography | 183

Abbreviations

KTU	*Die Keilalphabetischen Texte aus Ugarit*
KJV	King James Version
LXX	Septuagint
MT	Masoretic Text
NAS	New American Standard
NIV	New International Version
NLT	New Living Translation
NKJV	New King James Version
NRSV	New Revised Standard Version

Introduction

SOMETIMES, A LITTLE EXTRA Greek or Hebrew background can make a big difference to the average reader as we read God's word. It helps to know that in both languages, the same word (*shamaʿ* in Hebrew, *akouō* in Greek) can mean either "hear," "listen," "pay heed," or "obey." Knowing this can be extremely helpful—it puts you, the reader, in charge of deciding what the word means in any given verse.

It helps when reading in Revelation 10:6 that "there shall be no more *chronos*" to know that *chronos* can mean either "*time* shall be no more" (as the King James Version reads) or "there shall be no more *delay*." We see this in Matthew 24:48, where the wicked servant says, "My master *chronizei*," meaning "My master is delaying" or literally "taking-his-time."

It helps to know that the word *parrēsia* in the New Testament can mean confidence or boldness. It's the word for how Hebrews 4:16 says we can approach God's throne with confidence or boldness. But in Mark 8:32, it is used to say that Jesus first spoke of his coming death "plainly" or "openly." In Acts 28:31, any of these meanings would fit.

It helps to know that while the word *phōnē* in the New Testament normally means "voice," particularly when we are told that someone is speaking, there are eleven times in the book of Revelation where the word means "sound" or "noise" (4:5, 8:5, 9:9, 10:7, 11:19, 14:2, 16:18, twice in 18:22, and twice in 19:6). We see this meaning of the word very clearly in John 3:8, where Jesus says we hear the "sound" of the wind. We also see it in 1 Corinthians 14:7–8, where Paul speaks of the "sound" of flute, harp, and trumpet. So when we read in Revelation 8:5 about a plague accompanied by flashes of lightning, thunder, an earthquake, and *phōnai*, we can translate *phōnai* as either "noises" or "voices."

It also helps to know the options for the word "Lord/lord" in both Hebrew and Greek. In Hebrew, the word *baʿal* can mean either "lord," "master," "husband" (sorry, ladies!), *and* the Canaanite god Baal. So you could say, "YHWH is my *baʿal*" (meaning Master), but that created too much confusion. (See Hosea 2:16, which echoes that confusion.) Instead, the Hebrews called God *Adonai* ("my Lord"), while *adon* was also the standard respectful way to address someone as "sir." The same is true for the Greek word *kurios*. So when Jesus appears to Saul on the Damascus Road and Saul asks, "Who are you, Lord?", Saul could just as easily mean "Sir," since he obviously doesn't know yet who he is talking to. When strangers address Jesus as "*Kurios*," they may mean "Sir," or they may already mean "Lord."

None of these examples takes an entire chapter to discuss. However, there are quite a few more biblical words on which a lot more can be said to help you, the average reader, as you study God's word. I have chosen to explore at least sixty of them with you in the following chapters. Some of these words are used very few times (chapter 1 is about a word that is used only once!), so for them we need to go outside the Bible to help figure out their meaning. However, many of these words are used often in the Bible, but can vary greatly in their meaning. Often context will help you figure what the word means, as long as you know what the translation options are. That's where this book comes in.

My aim is to give you just enough added information from the Bible's original languages to help you figure out for yourself what these words mean, particularly at those times when you're in a Bible study, and somebody says, "My Bible says this, while your Bible says that!" You may be able to say, "The original word can be translated either way."

Now, sometimes the issue is not translation, but manuscript evidence (such as whether the ending of the Lord's Prayer is part of the Bible's original text or not). If the issue is how to trace the original text, or if the issue is grammar, you'll have to look elsewhere for help. Sometimes the margin of your Bible will explain the options.

There are far more biblical words than we can cover in this book (many of them have already been well covered elsewhere). That's why our final chapter is about how you can do word studies for yourself, even if you've never studied Greek or Hebrew. Hopefully, you'll know a little more of both languages by the time you finish this book. How freeing it is to dig deeper into the language of God's word than our English translations can take us! What a joy it can be! I hope you'll have some fun as we look deeper into God's word!

1

Count It All Dung!

DID THE WORD THAT Paul uses for "dung" in Philippians 3:8 really stink?

The plural of the Greek noun *skubalon* is used only once in the New Testament, but it is worth investigating what exactly Paul meant when he used it. In Philippians 3:8, Paul speaks of Jesus as the one "because of whom I have suffered the loss of all things, and count them as dung (King James's choice of words!), in order that I may gain Christ."

Strong words! But does *skubala* mean "dung," or does it mean something like "rubbish" or "garbage"? *Skubalon* is one of those broad words that can mean either option. Even King James English words like "dung" or "manure" do not always refer to intestinal solid waste. So allow me to use "dung" as shorthand for what is expelled from the large intestine, the literal basic meaning behind its use as a non-literal negative descriptive term. Perhaps Paul used this particular Greek word to express himself because its range of meaning was similar to this old English word.

Philo of Alexandria often uses the plural form *skubala* to refer to the refuse from the threshing of grain. "For to be able to distinguish what is necessary from what is *skubala*, and what is nutritious from what is not, and what is true from what is spurious, and what is useful fruit from a worthless root, not in the things which the earth bears but rather what the mind sprouts, is the most perfect virtue." (*On Dreams* 2:22) Philo also speaks of the job of the ox as "the cleansing of the piles of grain, and the separation of the *skubala* from the genuine and useful." (*On Virtues* 145)

Skubalon can also be used to mean "garbage" or "refuse." Sibylline Oracles 7.58: "You will be the miserable *skubalon* of war." Achilles Tatius 2.11.5: "He reviled the catch and threw it out as *skubalon* of the sea." Similar uses can be found in the Palatine Anthology: "leftovers" from dinner, "crumbs that fall from the table" (Ariston), the remains of a dead person (Philip of Thessalonika), and the wreckage of a ship (Hegesippus).

But in his book on *Questions and Answers in Genesis* (2:6, 2:7), Philo uses *skubalon* (singular) as the medical term for what is expelled after food is digested. He even speaks of the door in the side of Noah's ark as being the ark's rectum from which all of its bodily waste (*skubala*, plural) was expelled (2:6). Strabo refers to poor drainage in a city leading to "filth" collecting on the streets (*Geography* 14.1.37). And Clement of Alexandria (around AD 200) pairs *skubala* together with urine and other bodily waste products (*Christ the Educator* 3.11.65). He also says of women who have golden toilet pots, "I wish that for the rest of their lives they considered gold as worthy of *skubalōn*." (*Christ the Educator* 2.3.39) Indeed, Greek medical writers, who studiously avoid foul language, use *skubalon* to say what they mean when they speak of solid bodily waste.

Josephus speaks of how the besieged residents of Jerusalem were driven "to scour the sewers and old dunghills of cattle to use [eat] the *skubala* from them, and the things which they formerly could not bear the sight of now became food" (*Jewish War* 5:571). In an Egyptian papyrus scrap (Papyrus Fayum 119.7), a man named Gemullus tells his son that a donkey-driver bought some rotten (*sapron*) hay that was decayed so badly that it was *hōs skubalon* ("like dung"). *Skubalos* is even used as a personal name in some of the papyri, although it sounds like a derogatory nickname; it hardly seems have been a name given by loving parents, but the name may have been given to newborns who had been rescued from being cast into dungpiles. There is even a verb form, *skubalizein*, used in the *Apostolic Constitutions* (2.43.3) to describe how a troublemaker acts "as if he were handpicked by the devil *to treat* the church *like dung*" (or however one might choose to translate the thought).

Hesychius's Greek dictionary (around AD 500) defines *skubala* as meaning the same as *kopria* (= *kopros*), the undoubted Greek term for dung. In Sirach 27:4, *kopria* and *skubala* are paired as synonyms; as a sieve reveals the *kopria* in the wheat, so a person's words reveal the *skubala* within. Jerome translates the word in Philippians 3:8 into Latin as *stercora*, again, an unambiguous term for dung. And when Symmachus re-translates the passage where Ezekiel is commanded to bake his bread on human dung (Ezekiel 4:12, 15), he replaces the Septuagint's *kopros* with *skubala*, a passage where the meaning is beyond dispute.

We cannot be sure exactly what meaning Paul had in mind when he says he counts all things like dung, so that he may gain Christ. It was not an obscene word that he uses (obscenity is the topic of chapter 4), but it was strong language nevertheless, simply based on what the word means. And the range of meaning for the word he uses should lead us to reexamine how we regard all those values and obsessions of ours which Paul "trashes" (literally). Compared with the value of knowing Christ, everything else to which we devote our lives is "dung."

Do we truly believe that? And do we live like we believe it? To what extent are we like the famished besieged people of Jerusalem, digging through sewers and dungpiles to satisfy our souls? Can we bring ourselves to truly believe and live, controlled by the knowledge that compared to Christ, all of the rest is garbage, junk, even (as King James renders it) dung?

2

Iron Age Super Mom: Woman of Valor

"A woman of valor, who can find?" (Proverbs 31:10) The Hebrew word *ḥayil* (pronounce with a rough ḥ like in "Ḥanukkah") that is used in this verse is a rich value word, used 245 times in the Hebrew Bible. It is a word so broad that its meaning must be dictated by its context. It can mean monetary value. It can refer to the values of physical or military strength. It can mean "valor" in the sense of moral or personal worth.

The Iron Age Super Mom of Proverbs 31 is called a woman of *ḥayil*. The rest of that chapter spells out all the ways in which she is deemed to be a woman of valor or worth: brains, managerial skill, physical fitness, economic savvy, industriousness, moral wisdom, compassion, and love. At the end of the chapter (31:29), we find the expression to "do valiantly" (*ʿasah ḥayil*), found also in places such as Numbers 24:18 (subject: Israel) and Psalm 118:15 (subject: God). Iron Age Super Mom does more "valiantly" than any woman who can compare to her.

Ruth has a similar reputation among Bethlehem's leaders as a "woman of *ḥayil*" (Ruth 3:11, translated as "worthy" or "virtuous"); she is admired not only for her unselfish devotion to Naomi, but her courage to follow Israel's God and to trust God to provide for her, while being willing to work hard to make it happen. Boaz himself is described as a *gibbor-ḥayil* (Ruth 2:1), which means "warrior of valor" throughout Joshua and Judges, but here in a peaceful context is usually translated "man of great wealth." Likewise, in Ruth 4:11, Naomi's friends' wish for Boaz and Ruth is that they do/

make ḥayil (prosper, achieve wealth, or "do valiantly," the same phrase as in Proverbs 31:29).

Ḥayil is often used as a military word. We find dozens of references to *gibborē-ḥayil* (warriors of valor) and *anshē-ḥayil* (men of valor), where the emphasis is on military might and courage. In dozens of additional verses, the word means "army", a collection of power or force (Exodus 14:4—"Pharaoh and all his *ḥayil*"). In 2 Chronicles 14:7, the word is used two different ways: once to mean "army," and once to mean "valor" (!). In Psalm 33:17, we are told that a war horse cannot save by the greatness of its *ḥayil*. And of course, God can wield *ḥayil* that can overpower any human military power (Psalm 59:11).

Less often, *ḥayil* is used to mean other kinds of strength. In Genesis 47:6, Pharaoh says to Jacob about his sons, "If you have any men of *ḥayil* (competence or capability?) among them, put them in charge of my livestock." Similarly, Moses is advised to find men of *ḥayil* capable to decide cases that do not require his personal attention, a job that would not require muscle (see also 1 Chronicles 9:13). In a different sense, Isaiah 5:22 jokes about those who are "men of *ḥayil* (= heroes) in mixing malt liquor."

The expression "to gird on *ḥayil*" is unspecific as to whether it refers to strength, courage, endurance, or what exactly (1 Samuel 2:4; Psalm 18:33, 18:40). Similarly unspecific are Habakkuk 3:19, "YHWH my Lord is my *ḥayil*," and the famous line in Zechariah 4:6, "Not by *ḥayil*, not by *koḥ* (physical might), but by my Spirit, says the Lord." It is likewise unclear what kind of strength is meant where King Lemuel's mother says to her son, "Give not your *ḥayil* to women" (Proverbs 31:4). Joel 2:22 even tells us that the fig tree and the vine shall yield their *ḥayil* (richness or fruitfulness?).

But there are specific verses where *ḥayil* undoubtedly means "wealth," particularly in Job and in poetry. In 1 Kings 10:2, the Queen of Sheba comes with "a very great *ḥayil*." Is this an army, or is it more likely a display or collection of wealth? The author goes on to presumably specify the answer: "camels bearing spices and very much gold and precious stones." When Zechariah predicts that the *ḥayil* of all nations shall be gathered, he specifies wealth as what he means: "gold, silver, and garments in great abundance" (Zechariah 14:14). In Deuteronomy 8:17–18, Moses warns Israel not to say "the might of my own hand has earned me this *ḥayil*," because God is "the one who gives you the power to earn *ḥayil*." Psalm 62:10: "If *ḥayil* increases, do not set your heart on it."

Watch what *ḥayil* is paired with, if you want proof as to where *ḥayil* means "wealth." It is paired with "treasure" in Isaiah 30:6, Jeremiah 15:13 and 17:3, it is paired with "profit/gain" in Micah 4:13, it is paired with "spoil/plunder" in Isaiah 8:4, and it is paired with "abundance of riches" in Psalm 49:6. Zephaniah 1:13 says "their *ḥayil* shall become plunder." Psalm 49:11 declares that people "die and leave their *ḥayil* to others." "Wealth" is the meaning that makes the most sense in these examples.

Ḥayil: a most versatile word, the quintessential value word, covering a wide range of both what we humans value, and of what God values! It is a fitting adjective to describe Iron Age Super Mom, and all who are like her today. May God grant us to value what God values in Scripture: courage and strength to withstand dangerous threats, wealth (where dollars can provide for tangible human needs), heroic love, and faith to ultimately trust in God rather than in fallible earthly weapons or resources.

3

How Did *Agapē* Become the Ultimate Word for Love?

PAUL'S FAMOUS WORDS ON the Greek word *agapē* in 1 Corinthians 13 become the most eloquent definition of "love" in all human literature. But how did Paul and the New Testament faith community come to choose that word to mean the exalted kind of love of which Paul writes in this chapter? And what insights can we glean from digging deeper into his definition of that word?

In the Hebrew Bible, there was a generic word for love: *ahabah* and its verb form *ahab*. There were a few rarely used words for erotic love, *dod* (Proverbs 7:18) and *'ugabah* (Ezekiel 23:11). But the word that most closely resembles Paul's definition of *agapē* love is the word *ḥesed*, a word often translated "loving kindness" (King James) or "steadfast love" (Revised Standard) in our English versions.

Ḥesed is a combination of "love" and "loyalty." It is the word repeated in every line of Psalm 136: "for his lovingkindness endures forever." (See also famous lines such as Exodus 20:6, and Psalm 100:5 and 103:8.) *Ḥesed* is a love that never quits, a word that amazingly resembles the kind of love that Paul depicts in his divinely inspired essay on *agapē*. The resemblance is so striking that one might wonder whether *agapē* was the word used to translate *ḥesed* into Greek.

Surprisingly, no! The Greek version almost always uses the word "mercy" (*eleos*) to translate this Hebrew word, and absolutely never uses *agapē*. (The New King James agrees with this translation.) It would appear that *agapē* did not mean what it means for Paul at the time that the Septuagint was being translated (early to mid-200s BC).

Instead, the Greek version uses *agapē* and its verb form *agapaō* to translate the generic Hebrew word for love. *Agapaō* is used for romance, family love, love for neighbor (Leviticus 19:18, the Second Greatest Commandment), love for God (Deuteronomy 6:4–5, the Greatest Commandment), and love from God (Jeremiah 38:3 LXX = English 31:3 NRSV, "I have loved you with an everlasting love").

There is nothing remarkable about the noun *agapē* in any of its pre-Christian uses. In fact, *agapē* is used almost entirely simply for strong emotional attachment. Eleven of the nineteen times it is used in the Septuagint are in Song of Solomon. It is even used to describe the passion that propelled Amnon to sexually assault his half-sister Tamar (2 Samuel 13:15).

So what happened, then? It appears that *agapē* was chosen to convey the exalted form of love that Paul describes, because other words were too attached to other meanings. *Phileō* was the love Isaac had for Jacob's pot of stew (Genesis 27:4), and love for other foods (Proverbs 21:17, Hosea 3:1). It was also the standard verb for a kiss of greeting (fifteen out of thirty-three times in the Septuagint). Its noun form *philos* is the standard word for "friend" (John 15:13).

Storgē was used only for love within a family; Romans 1:31 speaks of those who are *a-storgoi*, "without family affection" (such as those who would abort or expose their children). *Erōs* was too exclusively associated with sex (Proverbs 7:18), and *aphrodisia*, a non-biblical word, was even worse (as Tina Turner asked, What's love got to do with it?).

Actually, *agapē* is only used twice anywhere in the first three Gospels: Matthew 24:12 ("the love of many will grow cold") and Luke 11:42 ("you neglect justice and the love of God"). *Agapē* is never used in the whole book of Acts (neither is the verb!). But the noun is used seven times in John's Gospel, seventeen times in John's epistles, and *seventy-five times* in Paul's letters. And the verb is used twenty-six times in the Synoptic Gospels, thirty-seven times in John's Gospel, thirty-one times in John's letters, and thirty-four times in Paul.

In 1 Corinthians 13, Paul takes a previously generic Greek term for love and loads it with new meaning. He says in 13:4 that love does not envy or show off, and is not "puffed up" (RSV: "arrogant;" NIV: "proud"). In 13:5, he says that love does not behave "shamefully" (most versions: "rude"). He says it "does not seek its own things" (RSV: "does not demand its own way;"

NIV: "is not self-seeking"), and is not "provoked" (as the NKJV puts it—the NLT and NRSV read "irritable").

Paul's last point in 13:5 is that love literally "does not reason/calculate the bad." In other words, it "thinks no evil" (NKJV) or "keeps no record of wrong" (NLT). In 13:6, Paul declares that love "does not rejoice at wrongdoing, but rejoices with the truth." In 13:7, Paul attributes four constant action verbs to love: it always "bears" (NIV: "protects"), "trusts," "hopes," and "endures."

In 13:8, Paul proclaims that love never "falls." That is, love never quits or goes obsolete. He compares the everlasting nature of love to spiritual gifts and knowledge, which will one day be abolished. In the end, Paul says in 13:13 that only faith, hope, and love will remain, but the greatest of these is love. That's why Paul writes in the very next verse (14:1), "Pursue love." The verb he uses here is the verb for "chase down" or "persecute" (!).

What a masterpiece portrait of love! Who can measure up to such love? If you think you do, you are deceiving yourself. People who come close to measuring up to this kind of love are an endangered species indeed, and only the Holy Spirit can make such love happen.

Agapē is an unconditional love that gives without expecting in return. It is a self-sacrificial love, the kind God showed us in what Jesus did for us on the cross—that is, if he really was bearing the penalty for our sin. (Which I believe he was.)

Finding the right word for such love in Greek was not easy. We still don't have the right word for it in English.

4

The Bible's Teaching on Obscene Language

Abusing God's name is profanity. But what does the Bible say about obscenity? And why the —— does it matter whether we use such language?

What exactly is obscene language is in the mind of each listener. Always has been, always will be. There are very few words on anyone's list that everyone considers to be indecent or obscene. Even the old King James Version uses as least two words that are still on my list of words that I won't say.

Paul features the Greek term *aischrologia* (shameful language) on a sin list in Colossians 3:8. In a parallel sin list in Ephesians 5:4, he uses *aischrotēs* (indecency) plus "*moron*-talk" plus *eutrapelia*, a word that has been translated "coarse jesting" (NKJV), "coarse joking" (NIV), and "vulgar talk" (NRSV), but may also be translated "buffoonery" or even simply "wittiness," as Aristotle uses the term to mean. It would appear that whether *eutrapelia* is bad or not all depends ultimately on the content thereof.

Unfortunately, we do not have a list of the words that Paul considered to be shameful. And if we did, it would be in Greek anyway. When I wrote my book *What's on God's Sin List for Today?*, I stated that the ancient writers have given us no such list. While technically that statement may still be true, today I would say that nevertheless, there *is* evidence from which we can piece together such a list. A superb resource on the subject is Jeremy Hultin's dissertation, *The Ethics of Obscene Speech in Early Christianity and Its Environment* (see bibliography).

THE BIBLE'S TEACHING ON OBSCENE LANGUAGE

There are certain Greek words that tend to be found only in the Old Comedy texts, in bawdy writers such as Aristophanes and Lucian, and on graffiti such as is found at Pompeii. These include verbs such as *binein* (the f-verb), *chezein* (the s-verb), *pygizein* (the verb for anal sex), and *laikadein* (the verb for oral sex, which the ancients viewed as worse than pederasty—Juvenal has Roman harlots say, "We would never dream of doing that to each other!"), plus the noun *prōktos* (from which we get "proctologist") and the less-than-decent terms for genitals, *posthōn* (male) and *kysthos* (female).

Plato, Aristotle, Plutarch, and most Greek writers after 400 BC tend to avoid such words. By contrast, Roman comics in Imperial times were fairly obscene. Martial is constantly using the Latin f-verb (*fūtuere*), and the nouns *mentula* (short for "Richard") and *cunnus* (= Greek *kysthos*).

Plato would have banned *aischrologia* entirely in his ideal Republic, because of its effects on those who hear it. Aristotle (like Jesus!) was more concerned about what such language revealed about the heart of the speaker. Cicero argued that there is nothing inherently evil in the sounds themselves. Nor can the evil be in the objects or actions spoken of, because there are other words that can be used for the same actions or objects; obscenity, he says, is "nowhere." Quintilian concurs: "no word is shocking (*turpis*) in itself ... if the thing meant is disgusting, it comes to be understood by whatever name it is called." (Quintilian, *Orator's Education* 8.3.55)

Hultin observes, "Greeks and Romans did not generally use obscene words to fill out speech," nor "in response to a sudden shock."[1] If one of the ancients banged their foot on a rock, they would pronounce a divine curse on it. Aside from the use of coarse language in comedy writings and plays, the most curious use of such language was in religious cults such as the festival of Demeter, where we are told that *aischrologia* was used to cheer the goddess with laughter. Also, in an addition to his *Dialogue of the Courtesans*, Lucian tells of a secret ceremony for women where priestesses whisper suggestions of adultery and crude descriptions thereof in their ears, while carrying vulgar replicas of genitals.

Incidentally, we are told that at Athens, there was indeed a list of forbidden epithets, but these were not crudities. Rather, they were slanders such as "shield-thrower" (coward) or "patricide," which were viewed as horrible names for which the speaker could be punished in court.

---

1. Hultin, *Ethics of Obscene Speech*, 11.

What about the Christian approach to obscene language? In *Didachē* 3:3 (around AD 95), it is argued that *aischrologia* leads to adultery. Likewise, popular preacher John Chrysostom (late AD 300s) declares that *aischrologia* and *eutrapelia* are the "chariot of fornication." Suggestive language suggests a behavior.

In Book 2 of his *Christ the Educator*, Clement of Alexandria has a chapter on *aischrologia*. He writes, "We ourselves must steer completely clear of all *aischrologia*, and those who resort to it we must silence with a sharp look, or by turning our face away, or by what is called a grunt of disgust, or by some pointed remark." (2.6.49) Clement quotes Jesus: "The things that come out of the mouth defile a person." Avoiding indecent language, he says, will prevent it from penetrating and injuring the soul. "If he who merely calls his brother a fool is liable to judgment, what sentence should be passed upon obscene conversation?" (2.6.50) "It is imperative, then, that we neither listen to nor look at nor talk about obscene things. And it is even more imperative that we keep free of every immodest action, exposing or laying bare any parts of our body improperly, or looking at its private parts." (2.6.51)

Clement teaches that Christ "has forbidden the too free use of certain terms, meaning to eliminate too free contact with immorality . . . we have shown that it is not the terms, or the sexual organs, or the marriage act, to which names not in common use describing intercourse are affixed, that we should consider obscene . . . It is only the unlawful use of these organs that is improper . . . In the same way, writings that treat of evil deeds must be considered *aischrologia*, such as the description of adultery or pederasty or similar things." (2.6.52) Here Clement concurs with pagan writers such as Isocrates: "Things that are shameful to do, do not consider these things to be OK (*kalon*) to speak." Similarly, Pseudo-Aristotle: "Guard against even speaking shameful deeds with shameful names." Pseudo-Plutarch likewise argues that a word is but a shadow of a deed.

What shall we conclude for our Christian behavior today? Ephesians 4:29 frames the issue well: "Let no rotten/putrid (*sapros*) word come out of your mouths, but only what is good (*agathos*) for a constructive purpose, so that the word may give grace to those who hear." Words send signals to those around us. Obscenity is designed to jab like a knife. Used too much, and it may cease to shock others, but will continue its corrosive effect on how we are heard by others. And sometimes, such as today's constant references to oral sex as a statement of disapproval, we may have no idea whom we are offending.

When a former senator was first criticized for saying "bulls—t" in a public speech in the early 1990s, his response was, "Shucks, that's just the way we talk back in Iowa." My response from the pulpit was to recall the words of Jesus: "The mouth speaks what the heart is full of" (Matthew 12:34). A constant flood of obscenities out of someone's mouth should be a warning about the condition of their heart.

5

What's Wrong with Getting Drunk, Paul?

What's wrong with getting drunk? Paul's one-word answer in Ephesians 5:18 is as hard to define in English as it is in Greek. "Be not drunk with wine, for that is—"dissipation"? (NKJV, NAS) Or is it "debauchery"? (NRSV, NIV) Most of us need a dictionary to understand either of these words, even though they are in English.

"Debauchery" (originally a French word) is defined by Webster as "extreme indulgence in sensuality." "Dissipation" is defined as "wasteful expenditure," from "dissipate," meaning "to cause to spread out or spread thin to the point of vanishing." So where does that leave us?

"Wherein is excess" (old KJV) is a little more understandable and concise than the other versions. "Because that will ruin your life" (NLT) may be less literal, but it is the easiest translation to understand and the closest to the meaning of the word that Paul uses.

Asōtia is the noun Paul uses to explain what's wrong with getting drunk. The noun form is used three times in the New Testament. In addition to the Ephesians passage, Paul warns in Titus 1:6 that church overseers should have children who are not open to accusations of *asōtia* or incorrigibility. In 1 Peter 4:3–4, Peter says that unbelievers are surprised that his readers do not join them in the flood of *asōtia* that he describes in the previous verse. He describes *asōtia* with a list of vices that includes three terms for alcohol abuse, plus a term for "licentiousness" (*aselgeiais*) that goes beyond mere fornication and adultery (see chapter 18).

Asōtia is also used twice in the Greek Old Testament. In Proverbs 28:7, it is used to translate "gluttony." And in 2 Maccabees 6:4, we are told that the Greeks filled the temple with *asōtia* and carousing (*kōmoi*, wild partying with both food and drink). The adjective form *asōtos* is used to describe the woman on the prowl in Two-Time Square in Proverbs 7:11, where the Hebrew says she is loud and "rebellious." To be an *asōtos* is to indulge so excessively that one destroys oneself.

Possibly the most famous use of this Greek root is in its adverb form (*asōtōs*) in the parable of the Prodigal Son (Luke 15:13), where we are told that the son squanders his share of his father's inheritance in living "riotously." While the older brother in the story claims that the money was spent on harlots, the point of *asōtōs* seems to be that the inheritance was wasted in a wild and reckless manner.

Uses of *asōtia* outside the Greek Bible yield much the same results. Commenting on this word in his *Theological Lexicon of the New Testament*, Spicq observes that "the *asōtos* not only wastes his goods, but loses his time, degrades his faculties and abilities, and consumes him."[1] Philo writes that the besotted, debauched (*asōtos*) life is "a threat to everyone" (*On the Contemplative Life* 1:47). Heraclitus says, "Charybdis is a good name for the insatiable, spendthrift debauchery of drinking bouts."

Testament of Judah 16:1, a line from a biographical fiction piece from the second century BC, applies this word specifically to wine. Here, Judah the patriarch warns, "Watch out for the limit of wine, for in it are four evil spirits: of lust, of feverish passion, of *asōtia*, and of sordid gain." A few sections earlier in the piece (14:1), Judah uses the exact same words and forms as Paul does in Ephesians 5:18: "Be not drunk with wine." His rationale is that too much wine confuses the mind by filthy thoughts (*rhuparois*—14:3); the spirit of error invades one's mind (14:8), causing one to become foul-mouthed and lawless.

The philosopher Epicurus, who is famous for his line that "the beginning and root of all good is the pleasure of the stomach," nevertheless declares, "When then we say that pleasure is the goal [of life], we do not mean the pleasures of profligates (*asōtōn*) . . . For it is not continuous drinking bouts and carousing, nor the [sexual] enjoyment of boys and women, nor of fish and other items carried on the extravagant [dinner] table, which produce a pleasurable life, but sober reasoning" (*Epistle to Menoeceus* 131–32).

---

1. Spicq, *Lexicon*, 1:221.

Most of the time, *asōtia* refers to excesses of food and drink; for sexual indulgence, other terms tend to be used. In the case of food, *asōtia* refers to gluttony in its most unhealthy form. Dio Cassius (75.15.7) describes a character named Plautianus as being "*asōtotatos* (the most debauched) of men, so much so that he both feasted himself and vomited at the same time, because of the load of foods and wine he was not able to digest." (In the next line, Dio tells us that this character was also a notorious pedophile who preyed on both genders.) Josephus says that once the emperor Vitellius "left the palace drunk after a debauched (*asōtos*) dinner" (*Jewish War* 4:651).

Exhausting one's resources is another common meaning. Papyrus Florentini 99.7 uses the verb form *asōteuesthai*, "to exhaust all of one's resources," to describe a son who spent all his money on harlots, like the Prodigal Son was accused of doing. Athenaeus (4.59–67) tells of several *asōtoi* who devoured their entire family inheritances irresponsibly, including one who sold his father's monuments (gravestones?) worth a thousand drachmae to finance his riotous lifestyle. Athenaeus states that such *asōtoi* were often punished by the Areopagus at Athens for such behavior.

The meaning of *asōtia* may be illumined further by comparing it to other vices and virtues. *Asōtia* is regarded as the opposite of *aretē* (virtue, moral excellence). In the *Tablet of Cebes*, *Asōtia* is a harlot accompanied by *Akrasia* (Lack of Self-Control), *Aplēstia* (Insatiability), and *Kolakeia* (Lasciviousness). In his *Nicomachean Ethic*, Aristotle declares *asōtia* to be the opposite of *aneleutheria* or "stinginess."

Asōtia gets paired with vices such as being *ataktos* (unruly) and *aselgēs* (licentious), and with *rhathumia* (laziness) and *kinaidia* (horribly obscene behavior, even by Greek standards). Both Spicq and Kittel theorize that *asōtia* originally meant "incurable," which is precisely what the expression *asōtōs echein* means, an expression that is close to our modern concept of "addiction." (Similarly, Clement of Alexandria claims that *asōtia* means "beyond salvation," and takes Paul's warning to the Ephesians as a reference to the "hopelessness of the drunkard.")

What a picture of the dangers of substance abuse! (Don't get the wrong idea! Paul is not singling out wine, as if it were OK to be drunk with beer, liquor, marijuana, or other mind-altering drugs. No, Paul is forbidding the use of any mind-altering substance to get high.) *Asōtia* may be described by our concept of "getting wasted." The word gives us a picture of someone pouring their resources down the drain on food, alcohol, and other indulgences, ruining their mind, health, and life in the process.

As I put it in chapter 5 of my book, *What's on God's Sin List for Today?*, the bottom line is that for Paul, getting drunk is a reckless, harmful form of excess. That's hard to say in just one word. But Paul did it. Too bad we don't have any one word in plain English that does the same trick.

6

Is Elohim Jehovah, or a Pantheon?

Elohīm means "plurality of gods" only when the verb is plural. But usually the verb or modifying adjective in the Hebrew Bible is singular, especially when the subject is the one true God, YHWH.

(YHWH is traditionally mispronounced "Jehovah." Clement of Alexandria in AD 200 tells us, using Greek letters to fill in the vowels, that it was actually pronounced "*Iaoue*" or "Yahweh." The copyists who preserved the Hebrew text throughout the first millennium AD would always read the word *Adonai* or "Lord" to avoid pronouncing God's sacred name. "Jehovah" is a combination of the vowels of *Adonai* and the Latin letters J and V that were used for the Hebrew letters *yod* and *waw*.)

As we will see, most of the time *Elohīm* means the Sum Total of Deity. This form is usually called the "plural of majesty," but it resembles certain other similar nouns with a plural meaning "sum total," include the nouns *ḥayyīm* (life), *mēsharīm* (fairness/equity), *betulīm* (virginity), *neʿarīm* (youth), and *zequnīm* (old age).

Only a *mono*theistic people like Israel would employ this meaning. In fact, out of all Semitic languages, this use of the word "God" in plural form to mean only one God is found only in Hebrew, and in Jewish Aramaic texts such as Daniel. You won't find a plural word for God used with such a meaning in pagan Aramaic, in Ugaritic (Canaanite), or in Akkadian (Babylonian).

IS ELOHIM JEHOVAH, OR A PANTHEON?

Several times in the Hebrew Bible it is clearly stated that YHWH = *Elohīm*. The best example is Isaiah 45:18: "For thus says YHWH, who created the heavens; he (singular) is *Elohīm*." Here are some more examples:

- Deuteronomy 4:35: "So that you might know that YHWH, he (singular) is the *Elohīm*; there is no other."
- 2 Samuel 7:28: "O *Adonai* YHWH (Lord YHWH), you (singular) are the *Elohīm*."
- 1 Kings 8:60: "All the peoples of the earth shall know that YHWH, he (singular) is the *Elohīm*; there is no other."
- 1 Kings 18:37: "So that this people may know that you (singular), YHWH, are the *Elohīm*."
- 2 Kings 19:15: "O YHWH, *Elohīm* of Israel . . . you (singular) are the *Elohīm*, you alone."
- Isaiah 45:5: "I am YHWH, and there is no other; besides me there is/are no *Elohīm*."
- We also have YHWH and *Elohīm* paired together as one compound name *thirty-seven times* in the Hebrew Bible, starting in Genesis 2:4.
- I did not count the numerous times we find expressions like Isaiah 43:3, "I am YHWH your *Elohīm*" or Deuteronomy 6:5, "You shall love YHWH your *Elohīm*."

Elohīm is the plural of the noun *eloah*, meaning "god" or "God." The singular form is used fifty-eight times in the Hebrew Bible, forty-one of those times in Job. The plural *elohīm* is used 2248 times. It is used 366 times with the definite article "the," most of these in the phrases "ark of the *Elohīm*," "house of the *Elohīm*," and "man of the *Elohīm*." In Exodus 21:6, 22:8, and 22:9, the language is ambiguous as to whether people must bring cases to "the God" or "the gods" (or "the judges," as some, such as the King James translators, might understand the latter option).

As I said at the very beginning of this chapter, there are some strong signals given in the text when *Elohīm* is intended to be singular: whenever *Elohīm* is the subject of a singular verb, or is modified by a singular adjective, pronoun, or participle. Some examples:

- Genesis 5:24: "Enoch walked with the *Elohīm*, and he was not, for *Elohīm* took (singular verb) him."

- Genesis 41:28 (and 25): "The *Elohīm* has shown (singular verb) what he is doing (singular participle)."
- Exodus 18:16: "the statutes of the *Elohīm* and his (singular suffix) laws."
- 1 Kings 18:24: "The *Elohīm* who answers by fire, he (singular pronoun) is the *Elohīm*."
- Nehemiah 8:6: "Ezra blessed YHWH, the great (singular adjective) *Elohīm*."
- Psalm 86:8–10: "There is no one like you (singular) among the *elohīm*, O *Adonai* . . . *You* (singular) *alone* are *Elohīm*."

Exceptions to the above rules are extremely rare, but here's the few I found. In both Genesis 20:13 and Genesis 35:7, the verb used with *Elohīm* is plural, although few would argue from context that multiple gods are the plural subject of the verb; in the Samaritan Pentateuch text of these verses, the verb is singular, although one might dispute whether the plural is a corruption, or the singular is a "correction." In the phrase "living God" in Deuteronomy 5:26 and 1 Samuel 17:26, the adjective "living" is plural. And in 1 Samuel 28:13, the witch at En-dor says to Saul, "I see *elohīm* coming up (plural participle) from the earth." (The King James Version takes this to be an actual plural.)

So when does *elohīm* refer to gods (plural)? The King James translates the word this way 215 times. Deuteronomy 10:17 gives us an unusual case where both singular and plural meanings are juxtaposed in the same breath: "For YHWH your *Elohīm* is *Elohīm* (God) of *elohīm* (gods)." In Exodus 12:12, "all the *elohīm* of Egypt" refers to multiple pagan gods, as do the sixty-four times the phrase "other (plural adjective) *elohīm*" is used. The phrase "sons of *Elohīm*" is used only three times, all in Job; the meaning can be arguably singular or plural.

Finally, Psalm 8:5 and Psalm 82:1 and 82:6 are worthy of attention. Psalm 8:5 is the lone instance where the King James Version translates *Elohīm* as "angels," which is peculiar, in that "God" makes perfectly good sense here. As for Psalm 82, the context seems to fit the meaning "judges" as in Exodus 21:6 and 22:8–9 above, although evil heavenly powers may be in view.

In addition, there is the common Semitic word *Ēl* for "God/god," the plural of which always means "gods (plural)." In the Hebrew Bible, the plural refers to gods other than YHWH in Exodus 15:11 ("Who is like unto thee, O YHWH, among the gods?"), Job 41:25 ("the *ēlīm* are afraid"), Psalm 29:1, Psalm 58:1, and Psalm 89:6, among other examples. In such passages, in addition to similar passages that use the word *Elohīm* such as Psalm 138:1 and Psalm 82, pagan gods (or possibly lesser angelic powers) are referenced, without the author recognizing them as genuine deities who can be rightfully compared to the one true God.

The evidence demonstrates that the biblical faith was truly monotheistic: there is only one God, known alternately as *Elohīm* and as YHWH. There is only one God, not two. Our friends, the Latter-day Saints, do not accept these conclusions. They are not truly monotheistic; they claim to be monolatrous, that is, they claim to worship only one God, although limitless other gods have existed and do exist theoretically in LDS theology. However, there is confusion as to exactly which God the LDS do worship. Suddenly, the oft-denied doctrine of the Trinity begins to make more biblical sense.

7

Creation and How It Happened

How did creation happen? Is there a special word for what God did? At what taxonomic level did God create life? And how long did it take?

Only one being in this universe can create out of nothing. The rest of us must create out of previously existing material. Even if we create a new idea or object of art or intellectual property, we did not create the ingredients. (We could even question whether we create new ideas, or simply discover them; Ecclesiastes says there is "nothing new under the sun.")

The Hebrew Bible has a verb for it: *bara'*, to create out of nothing. We find this verb used forty-eight times, mostly in Genesis (eleven times), Psalms (six times), and Isaiah (seventeen times, mostly in chapters 40–45). (Beware of homonyms with very different meanings!) God is always the subject. *Bara'* is different from *yatzar*, to make from previously existing material, like a potter creating objects from clay. *Yatzar* is the word used in Genesis 2:7 for God making humans out of the dust of the earth. Still one more word for "create" is the generic *'asah*, to do or make. Both *'asah* and *bara'* are used for the totality of creation in Genesis 2:4, *bara'* being the more specific of the two.

What else does God create-out-of-nothing? Exodus 34:10 announces to the Hebrews in the desert that God will create unprecedented wonders. In Numbers 16:30, Moses warns that God is about to create one of those wonders: the earth will swallow up his opponents. In Psalm 51:10 (Hebrew 51:12), David cries, "Create in me a clean heart, O God!" Psalm 102:18 predicts that "a people yet to be created (= born) may praise the Lord." Isaiah

41:20 predicts that God will again create unprecedented events. Isaiah 45:7 declares that God creates both welfare (*shalom*) and harm or bad (*raʿ*, a word that we will explore in chapter 26). In Isaiah 54:16, God says, "I have created the destroyer." And in Jeremiah 31:22, God predicts that he will create one more new thing: "a woman protects a (grown) man."

Note that in Genesis 1, *baraʾ* is only used for the initial creation of heaven and earth on the first day, for the creation of animal life in the sea and air on the fifth day, and for the creation of humans on the sixth day. One could imply that God uses the elements from these creative acts to make the rest of what exists. In fact, on the third and sixth days, God commands the *earth* to bring forth plants and vertebrates. If I were inclined to believe in macro-evolution (which I am not), I would use these commands as biblical support.

We are told that God creates organisms according to their "kind" (*min*), a word that is used thirty-one times, almost entirely in the creation account, in the worldwide flood account, and the kosher animal passages in Leviticus 11 and Deuteronomy 14. In the latter passages, "species" fits the context best, but in Genesis, I suggest a higher taxonomic level.

Micro-evolution within a genus or species is hard to deny, such as the common descent of all species of sunfish. But macro-evolution that turns a tunicate into a fish, a fish into a frog, or a land mammal into a whale, would require so much change that only an intelligent Creator could make it happen. So my theory is that *min* refers to a genus within which its members are genetically close enough to interbreed. You can cross a lake trout and a brook trout, but not a trout and a bass; such "kinds" would require super-natural intervention to produce.

Look at the so-called Cambrian explosion. At its earliest end, the fossil record suddenly goes from the tiniest, simplest organisms to a wild number of phyla, with complex creatures like the trilobite suddenly appearing out of nowhere. This does not fit the model for gradual evolution, and it's a shame that most public school students are not given this information, because that would be creationism, one of the rare absolute evils in the belief system of relativists.

(Francis Collins is the only evolutionist who raises questions not yet answered by creationists, such as how to explain seemingly vestigial DNA. Other evolutionists fail to engage the scientific issues raised by creationists.)

What about the time frame for the biblical creation? Here, biblical inerrancy proponents (of which I am one) can agree to disagree. The literal 144-hour creation framework is said to be what the Bible really means, both by conservatives who believe it, and by liberals who reject it as foolish. It is argued that *yom* always means twenty-four-hour day, but one might ask how long the seventh day was; has God rested from creation or not? And how long is the Day of the Lord?

Others theorize that creation did not happen in six days, but was revealed in six days. This would include John Walton's cosmic temple theory (in his book *The Lost World of Genesis One*—see bibliography), which I find to be faithful and well-argued, but unconvincing for me. Walton's theory affirms that God creates all from nothing, but that the six days are actually about God organizing it all into the parts of God's cosmic temple.

Meredith Kline, one of my professors at Gordon-Conwell, offered us in class another version of the six-day revealing of creation: the framework hypothesis. Kline observes that plants are created on the third day, but the heavenly bodies are not created until the fourth day. He sees the order of the six days as not chronological, but topical. He sees the first three days as creation-kingdoms: the heavens, air and water, dry land and plants. During the second three days, God creates the kings who rule those realms: heavenly bodies, air and water creatures, and land mammals, including the human being, the creature appointed to rule them all.

Another option is the so-called "day-age" theory. One can see an account of gradual creation in Genesis 1, similar to what a secular scientist would suggest. It starts with an event like the Big Bang, where light and matter come into existence. The atmosphere forms, then the continents and plant life, then we capture the moon into our orbit, then aquatic life and flying insects (Pennsylvanian period?), then animals of the Jurassic and Cenozoic periods, with a pronounced break between these and the appearance of a creature made in the image of God. Each of us must allow God to speak to us as to which approach is the most faithful to God's word.

Implications: First, we are taught to believe that creation is good, because it is produced by God. (Tertullian's jab at those rascally Gnostics was that they reject the goodness of creation, but they have to hijack the Creator's water to baptize their converts!)

The other implication I find is that for years, I have taught my confirmation students that you are stuck with either a God who always existed, or matter that has always existed. You can worship God, or worship matter. Those are the options. To me, it is more logical that matter owes its existence to a higher power, specifically, the One first revealed in the Hebrew Bible.

8

Firmament: Dome or Atmosphere?

WHAT IS THE "FIRMAMENT" in the Genesis creation account? Is it a solid dome over the earth, as some claim? Or is Genesis talking about what we call the atmosphere?

The Hebrew word *raqiʿa* (most often translated "firmament") is used nine times in Genesis 1. It is also used twice in Psalms, five times in Ezekiel, and once in Daniel. The *raqiʿa* is the focal point of the second day of creation: "Let there be a *raqiʿa* in the midst of the waters" to separate the waters above from the waters below, "and God called the *raqiʿa* Sky/Heaven." In Psalm 19:1, the *raqiʿa* and "the heavens" are equated, paired there as poetic synonyms. In Psalm 150:1, God's *raqiʿa* is paired poetically with "his sanctuary." Daniel 12:3 pairs this same *raqiʿa* with the domain of the stars.

Ezekiel's use of *raqiʿa* may or may not refer to the same heavenly part of creation. In the context of his vision of what almost appear to be spaceships, Ezekiel sees a *raqiʿa* (without the definite article "the" when it is first mentioned), with a throne above it, someone seated on it, and a voice that comes from there (Ezekiel 1:22–26, 10:1). Whether or not this is meant to be the universal heavenly canopy created in Genesis 1 is not entirely clear.

The use of the Greek *stereōma* and the Latin *firmamentum* to translate *raqiʿa* has led to the persistent claim that what God creates above the earth on the second day of creation is a solid dome. This has led to two different ways to understand the language used here. One is to conclude that that the biblical narrator and audience were hopelessly prescientific slobs who really believed that the sky was a solid dome. The other approach is to understand the language as poetic and based on appearances, much as even modern scientists may refer to Mother Nature and sunrise.

Claims that the ancient Semitic world believed in such a dome separating the earthly and heavenly domains have been debunked by cuneiform scholars W. G. Lambert and Wayne Horowitz. One must travel several centuries after Genesis to the Greeks to find belief in a solid dome over the earth, and even this turns out to be one of several concentric solid spheres. It is perhaps this Greco-Roman belief that influenced the translations of the Septuagint and Vulgate toward the notion of a "firmament." Yet even by the time of Basil, Christian scholars began to question how solid that object that separates us from space really was. So the notion of "firmament" as the way to translate *raqiʿa* is the result of bad Greco-Roman science.

But there is a better way to translate *raqiʿa*. The better option is to call it an "expanse." The reason why is to be found in the meaning of the verbal root on which the noun is based. The verb *raqaʿ*, used eleven times in the Hebrew Bible, means to hammer thin, to stamp, and/or to spread. It is used for the manufacture of gold leaf in Exodus 39:3. In Numbers 17:4, Eleazar hammers bronze censers into a covering for the ark. In 2 Samuel 22:43, David sings, "I crushed them; I stomped (or spread?) them like the mud of the streets." Psalm 136:6 says that God "spread the earth upon the waters" (similarly, Isaiah 42:5 and 44:24). Isaiah 40:19 speaks of an artisan "overlaying" an idol with gold. Jeremiah 10:9 refers to "beaten" silver. And Ezekiel 6:11 and 25:6 both speak of "stomping" one's feet.

Those who believe the *raqiʿa* to be a solid dome point to the verb's use in metallurgy as evidence that the "firmament" is to be understood as a hard metal dome or vault. The one verse lending support to this argument is Job 37:18: "Can you, like him, *spread out* the skies, hard as a molten mirror?" (NRSV). But almost every word in this verse is open to being read differently. A better translation might be, "Can you, like him, spread out the clouds, strong (or mighty), like a display that has been poured out?"

There is less about solidity in this verbal root *raqaʿ*, than there is about thinness. *Raqaʿ* means to spread out material very thin. So "expanse" becomes a far superior translation for *raqiʿa*, whether or not one chooses to see that expanse as solid or otherwise. We don't need to see the biblical picture of the sky as if it were a dome with windows to hold back an ocean of water from above. "Windows" and the *raqiʿa* never appear together, and the language of "windows" is arguably not intended to be literal. As Younker and Davidson write, "One of the great ironies in recreating a Biblical cosmology is that scholars have tended to treat figurative usages as literal (such as Psalms and Job), while treating literal passages, such as Genesis, as figurative."[1]

Could one not see the atmosphere as that expanse or thin separation that God has created between earth and space? At the risk of being accused of reading into the Bible what one wants to find there, I would suggest that "expanse" is far more linguistically sound, consistent with the biblical uses of the word, and both scientifically and theologically tenable. Such an approach also avoids condescension; it shows far more respect for the biblical authors. You know, what they say is sometimes more profound than what they themselves could have grasped.

---

1. Younker and Davidson, "Dome," 56.

9

Sea Monsters in Genesis?

ON THE FIFTH DAY of the Genesis creation narrative (Genesis 1:21), we are told that God created the "great sea creatures" (*tannīnīm*). While there is a tendency to see these like the NRSV does as "monsters" or mythological creatures, my default setting is to see them as real. Which leads to the question, "What exactly were they?"

This is not to say that the term *tannīn* is never used mythologically. There is actually a range of creatures to which it refers. In the Hebrew Bible, it refers five times to serpents (Exodus 7:9, 10, 12; Deuteronomy 32:33; Psalm 91:13), the clearest being where Moses turns his staff into a serpent. But all of these clearly refer to a dry-land context. In Psalm 148:7, the creatures appear to be marine, the same as in Genesis 1:21.

Curiously, the Septuagint translates *tannīn* as *drakōn*, "dragon," everywhere except Genesis 1:21. In Genesis, context seems to be what leads the Greek translation to use the word *kētos*, a word often rendered "whale," but whose semantic range covers all sorts of sea "monsters." The Liddell-Scott lexicon of ancient Greek defines *kētos* as "any sea-monster or huge fish." Aristotle refers to "the *delphis* (dolphin), the *phalaina* (whale), and the rest of the *kētē*" (plural of *kētos*). In Homer's Odyssey, the term is used for "seals." *Kētos* is used three times in the Septuagint to refer to mythological chaos monsters in Job, and it is used for the "great fish" (*dag gadol*) in Jonah (and as cited in a quote from Jesus in Matthew 12:40).

Going back into Ugaritic, the Canaanite ancestor of Hebrew, the *tnn* root is mythological. It is used the same way in Isaiah 27:1 and 51:9,

SEA MONSTERS IN GENESIS?

where the *tannīn* is paired with Rahab and Leviathan (Ugaritic *Ltn*). In Canaanite culture, these were divine "chaos monsters." In Isaiah, these are demythologized characters like our Mother Nature. But underneath these characters must be real biological prototypes; indeed, the Leviathan of Job 41 has been hypothesized to be the crocodile "on steroids." So what creature lies behind the *tannīn*?

Because the linguistic root gives us no further clues, all we can do is make a few careful guesses. One strong candidate, in my opinion, is the sea creature that the Assyrians called the *naḫīrū*. (Search online for Steven Lundström, "The Hunt is on again! Tiglath-pileser I's and Aššur-bel-kala's nāḫirū-Sculptures in Assur.") Two Assyrian kings boasted that they caught one of these creatures, which they nicknamed the "horse of the sea." Because one Assyrian king says he received "horns" or "teeth" (Akkadian *šin*) from this creature as tribute, it could have been a narwhal (as suggested by Assyriologist Leo Oppenheim), although today the narwhal exists only in the Arctic. It also could have been a swordfish. The *Ugaritic Textbook* identifies this creature (*anḫr*) as a dolphin, but in the one Canaanite text where it is used (*KTU* 1.5.I.15), it is paired with "the lion of the wild;" a dolphin hardly seems to fit as a lion's ocean counterpart. The meaning of *naḫīrū* seems to be "blower" or "snorter" (connected to the word for "nostril" in Job 41:20 and 41:12 in the Hebrew), pointing to some sort of monstrous sea mammal. The sperm whale and the orca have also been prominently suggested.

One more wild suggestion: because the Hebrew *tannīn* seems to be a serpent when it refers to a land creature, might it be a giant squid when it refers to a sea creature? We may never know. Perhaps the word is meant to point us to a whole category of monstrous sea creatures. But my conviction is that Genesis 1:21 is not talking about some mythological chaos monster. No, the creatures in question (plural) were created-out-of-nothing by God (*bara'*), and God declares them to be "good." Which means that they are highly unlikely to be mythical personifications of chaos.

10

Managing God's Masterpiece

Jesus never spoke one word about conserving the environment. But I firmly believe it is an insult to the Creator to trash the Creator's masterpiece. From the rain forests of Oregon, to the spring-fed streams of the Missouri Ozarks, to the prairie grass of Iowa, I see God's reflection everywhere in the beauty of creation, and I want to keep it that way. Because I am a "conservative," it is only logical for me to want to conserve God's creation.

I first penned my thoughts on God's word and the environment several years ago in the online version of the *Presbyterian Outlook* ("Conserving God's Masterpiece"). Since this piece is no longer available online, I would like to share those thoughts again here. In addition, I would like to dig deeper into the meaning of the two key verbs in the creation mandate, words that have been misunderstood both by those who would take them as permission to abuse creation, and by those who would condemn these words for that very same (mistaken) reason.

God has charged us to manage the earth faithfully. The term "subdue" (*kabash*) in Genesis 1:28 is used a total of fifteen times in the Hebrew Bible; its basic meaning is to bring hostile forces under control, such as the inhabitants of Canaan (Joshua 18:1), or to bring people into subjection as slaves (Nehemiah 5:5, Jeremiah 34:11). One memorable verse is where Haman falls on the couch to beg Queen Esther for his life, and the king roars, "Will he even *assault* the queen in my presence?" (Esther 7:8 NRSV). Another remarkable verse is where Micah rejoices over the day when God will "subdue" our iniquities (Micah 7:19).

The term "have dominion" (*radah*) is used a total of twenty-two times in the Hebrew Bible; its basic meaning is to manage with authority, like Solomon ruling his empire (1 Kings 5:4). Likewise, Psalm 72:8 says of the king, "May he *rule* from sea to sea." Surprisingly, in Psalm 68:28, it is Benjamin that "rules" the other tribes. Israelites are forbidden to "rule" their slaves with harshness (Leviticus 25:43, 25:46, 25:53). In Leviticus 26:17, Israel is warned that if they sin, their enemies shall "rule" over them. And in Jeremiah 5:31, we are told that the prophets prophesy falsely, and the priests "rule" at their direction.

These two verbs in the creation mandate teach that we are not to let nature tyrannize us, but that we must exercise faithful management thereof for the good of humankind. Extreme environmentalism would demand that we sacrifice human lives and health on a mass scale for the dubious good of an earth that hardly merits human sacrifice. God's word does not give us license to squash whatever threatens the comfort or convenience of our lifestyle, but it does teach us that we must subdue threats to human life, because we care for those who are made in God's image.

Sadly, some have misunderstood the creation mandate as a command to run roughshod over creation, to bulldoze it to death as we see fit, as if we had better ideas than the Creator, like the old cartoon of a Corps of Engineers commander on a project saying, "This is what God would have done if he'd had Federal funds." When I was a teenager, I had a bumper sticker that opposed the proposed Meramec Dam, which would have flooded miles of beautiful river, plus one of the largest caves in Missouri. I have always passionately opposed the mindless dredge-it-and-dam-it approach to God's creation.

I seek to live a lifestyle that does as little damage to this planet as possible. Our family recycles, even when it is cheaper or more convenient not to do so. We drive two Hondas that get forty to forty-five miles per gallon on the highway. Our gas/electric bill varies from $80 to $200 per month. We have a microscopic carbon footprint compared to Al Gore's.

But the only reason I conserve is because I believe God has put only so much coal and oil in the ground, which we have no right or excuse to waste. I refuse to buy into the global warming hysteria. The earth may or may not be getting warmer, and we may or may not be contributing much to it.

But even if it were all true, who is to say that our present sea level is God-ordained? Why not go back to its original level—whatever that was? And although I hate to let go of plants and animals that are threatened with extinction, who is to say whether God insists that we preserve all species that now exist at any and all costs, seeing that God either allowed or planned that many of those species would become extinct before the human race came into being?

Much as we do well to assist endangered species that are poorly adapted for survival, to prioritize them over human life and health is downright idolatry, to set them up as false objects of worship. That is, unless we concede to human beings the right to make such judgment calls as a part of our management responsibility over creation. But if we concede to humans the inalienable right to exercise such responsibility, then the floor is open to debate about whether Genesis's commands to prioritize human life should outweigh other needs.

One problem with environmental extremism is that it depends on blind faith in a "science" that is a moving target and is therefore quickly outdated. "Science" is treated as God's word until proven to be otherwise, and all contrary evidence is twisted and tortured to make the evidence fit the scientist's political preconceptions. But if today's "science" can be so rapidly debunked by tomorrow's science, how can we base divine imperatives on it?

Sadly, today's environmental extremism is exhibiting the worst traits that it condemns in others. It uses apocalyptic scare tactics that would make any Bible prophecy fanatic blush. People who would never invade our bedrooms to dictate anyone's moral behavior, want to impose environmental Sharia on us. They bully us into buying light bulbs with mercury in them to "save the earth," thus tripling the toxic waste in our trashcans. (Go figure!) They want to ban American oil drilling in the Gulf of Mexico, but they don't care if Cuba, Mexico, Brazil, or China drills there.

Seriously, if we really want to save the planet, we should ban lawn mowing and drive-throughs, both of which waste huge amounts of fuel. (I don't do drive-throughs, and would be glad to replace lawns with prairie grass or ivy.)

Our desire to faithfully care for God's masterpiece gains credibility when we avoid tying it to questionable claims of a science that may soon prove itself wrong, and when we avoid preaching, or imposing on others, what we ourselves do not practice.

11

How Equal Was Adam's Mate?

WAS ADAM'S MATE INTENDED as a subservient assistant, or an equal partner? A lot hangs on the meaning of an innocent-looking Hebrew preposition in Genesis 2:18, where God says, "It is not good for the human to be alone. I will make for him a help(er) *negedō*." What this little word means is foundational for the relationship of male and female in biblical theology.

The word *neged* is used 143 times in the Hebrew Bible. Its basic meaning is "face to face," from which it branches out into a range of meanings. It is used in Psalm 23:5: "You prepare a table before me, *right-in-the-face-of* my enemies." Eleven times in Nehemiah 3 it refers to points on Jerusalem's wall "opposite/next to" a particular reference point on the map. It is used similarly seven times in Ezekiel, including one place where a door was "opposite/facing" or "across from" another door (Ezekiel 40:13). The word is used thirty-six times in the Psalms, either with someone's "eyes" as its object, meaning "in my/your/their presence," or it can convey this meaning without the term "eyes," as in Psalm 51:3, "My sin is ever *before me*." Likewise, in Ruth 4:4, Boaz urges Naomi's closest kin to buy her land *in the presence of* the elders and all who are sitting in the gate: do the transaction "face-to-face" with everyone on the scene. Likewise, God declares that David's wives will be violated by another man in an "in-your-face" divine action "*before* all Israel and *before* the sun" (2 Samuel 12:12). Psalm 10:5 declares that God's judgments are so high above the wicked that they are far "from his face" (*minnegedō*).

While *neged* is often used to express the general idea of presence or sight, some of these verses clearly express the notion of "facing" directly across from the object of the word, a meaning which most closely approximates the root meaning of the word. In Joshua 3:16, Israel crosses the dried-up Jordan River at a point "opposite Jericho." Three times in 1 Chronicles (5:11, 8:32, 9:38) we are told that a family lives "alongside" or "opposite" another group as a point of reference. Such a meaning of "directly opposite" is echoed in the use of this word in Genesis 2:18.

God declares that the male human being needs a companion who is a point-by-point counterpart to himself. An animal will not do. A robot will not do. Any being that is a less-than-equal companion will not do. What is needed is a person who corresponds to the man almost like a mirror image, someone of whom he can say, "Bone from my bone and flesh from my flesh!" Not a clone, to be sure; if two of us are identical, one of us is not necessary. What is needed rather is someone who is a perfect match, who sees their partner eye-to-eye, on the same level, who corresponds with their partner at almost every point.

Such is the image that God gives us of the intended one-flesh partnership between male and female, hinging on that one little word *neged*. The language here does not resolve the debate over gender equality and male leadership, but it certainly provides major fuel for the discussion. I think it is no small detail that the decree that the man shall "rule" (*yimshal*) over his wife is located within a divine curse (Genesis 3:16), and is either a prediction of evil, or is part of the curse itself being pronounced by God. Such in my view does not appear to have been God's original intent. I and others with me long for a return to the time before the curse, where relations between male and female appear to have been characterized by joyful mutuality, face to face on a level with each other, matched at almost every point.

12

Methuselah: Man of Vitality

What does the name Methuselah mean? And how do we make sense out of the vast number of years he is reported to have lived?

As Richard Hess, Ephraim Speiser, and others have demonstrated, the names on the genealogies in Genesis 4–5 are far older than even names like Abram that date to the patriarchal age. One name worthy of investigation is the name of the longest living man in Genesis.

Methuselah (Genesis 5:25–27) is generally reckoned to be traceable to an Akkadian (Assyro-Babylonian) original *Mutu-she-laḫ*, "Man of *Laḫ*". But what do we do with the mystery word on the end? It has been suggested that the name should be translated "Man of the Spear." But I have a better suggestion, based on a rare Hebrew word found in Deuteronomy 34:7.

We are told in the postscript to Moses's life that Moses lived to be 120 years old, yet at the time he died, "his *lēḫ* was not diminished." The Greek and Latin translate the word as if it were *leḥi* or "jaw," leading the Greek version to read "his jaw was not deteriorated," and the Latin version to read "he had not lost his teeth."

Our Bibles translate this word as "vigor" or "life force." The word *lēḫ* literally means "sap," that is, the moisture that characterizes a living tree as opposed to a dead one. The related adjective is used for "fresh" bowstrings to tie up Samson (Judges 16:7–8), "fresh" grapes (Numbers 6:3), "fresh" wooden rods (Genesis 30:37), and "green" (as opposed to dry) trees (Ezekiel 17:24, 21:3).

Used here at the end of the Torah to describe what Moses (who was a human being rather than a plant or a tree) still had, "vitality" seems to be a good word to translate this word. And herein, I believe, lies the clue to the meaning of Methuselah's name. Methuselah = *Mutu-she-laḥ* = "Man of Vitality," an appropriate name for the reportedly longest-lived guy on the list. (Genesis 4, by the way, makes no mention of ages for the descendants of Cain.)

But now, how do we accept the Bible's word on the subject as anything other than fiction? We have no hard evidence for humans who have lived longer than the outside limit of 120 years suggested by Genesis 6:3. And yet, even today's science has only soft-tissue tools for determining the age of a human for whom bones and teeth are fully developed. How would we recognize the remains of a 900-year-old human if we found them?

There is the young earth theory to explain large ages in Genesis, suggesting that earth's atmosphere was thicker before the Flood, which would have lessened the amount of cosmic radiation which accelerates aging. While I am skeptical of the claim that conditions in the universe are the same as they've always been, I am also skeptical of claims that they are radically different, unless such claims are accompanied by evidence. To substantiate a thicker atmosphere in ancient times that screened out much more radiation than the atmosphere we have at present would for me require more evidence than we have, although I would welcome such evidence if it could be found.

I have a different suggestion, which I offer as wild speculation, a theory that is admittedly questionable, but better than any other explanation out there. I take a clue from the Assyrian and Sumerian King Lists, the closest parallels we have to Genesis 5 in the biblical world. These lists also testify to large ages before the Flood, ages that dwarf the Bible's ages by comparison. The oldest character on the Sumerian list is Enmenluanna (43,200 years old), but the runner-ups include Dumuzi and Alalgar (36,000), and Alulim and Enmengalanna (both 28,800). Both in Genesis and on the King Lists, the ages go way down after the Flood (on the King Lists, they go down to 1,500, 1,200, and 900–600).

(By the way, the modern consensus of both liberal and conservative scholars alike is that the genealogies in Genesis 5 and 11 are selective. They contain gaps. X is often not the immediate father of Y, but is Y's ancestor, perhaps several generations removed. There are exactly ten generations between Adam and Noah, and between Noah and Abraham. If we take the chronology strictly, Noah would have lived until Abraham was sixty years old. Therefore, most Bible-believing Christians no longer try to do the math to date the creation of Adam to 4004 BC.)

Kenneth Kitchen[1] does some tentative speculation on what can explain these large ages, using evidence from the Sumerian King List, where two notes in the margin indicate that the scribe was multiplying years of a king's reign by sixty (their numbering system was based on sixty). In fact, the large ages on the Sumerian king list divide easily by 600. Kitchen tries arbitrarily dividing the Genesis pre-Flood ages by five, and gets "normal" dates for each man's first child (all except Noah), and high but not-so-high ages at death. Kitchen concedes that in the Bible we are not dealing with reigns of kings or dynasties, but of individuals.

Taking a clue from Kitchen, what if we tried dividing those numbers by six? One possible reason for such large ages may be that numbers which were originally base ten were being read as base sixty. (See John Walton's article, "The Antediluvian Section of the Sumerian King List and Genesis 5" in the bibliography.) Such an approach could help explain the extreme ages in the text, while taking the narrative seriously as a truthful account of still record-busting ages for genuine pre-historic figures.

Yes, the weakness of my suggestion is that it may give the impression that the Bible's figures are in error. But biblical inerrancy has always insisted that the hypothetical original texts are what we hold to be authoritative and trustworthy. When God allows texts to depart from the original, God provides clues to help us reconstruct the original. Such reconstructions should not be sought lightly, but only for the strongest reasons. I would imagine that if Hodge and Warfield, the patriarchs of biblical inerrancy, were available for comment, they might well approve the theory that I am suggesting.

"Man of Vitality"—what better name for a man who lives longer than anyone in historic or prehistoric times? Yet Isaiah 65:22 promises that when God creates a new heaven and a new earth, our days will be "like the days of a tree" (presumably a bristlecone pine rather than a Bradford pear!). And because of the resurrection of Jesus Christ, we have reason to believe that this promise is a huge understatement aimed at an audience who could barely conceive of life in all its fullness that will last forever.

---

1. Kitchen, *Reliability of Old Testament*, 445–47.

13

The Ancient Flat Earth: A Modern Lie

PEOPLE IN BIBLICAL TIMES believed that the earth was flat? It's a modern lie, designed to depict the ancients as too backward for us to listen to. We call this "chronological snobbery," and in this case, even the premise is woefully exaggerated. It is amazing how much was known about the size and shape of the earth at this time.

For all the confusion of the ancients about the centrality of the earth versus the sun (which we will grant), Ptolemy spoke for the science of his day (circa AD 150) when he declared that the earth was a sphere. He arrives at this hypothesis using logic that no doubt had been formulated by Phoenician sailors for centuries: "whenever we sail toward mountains or any high places from whatever angle and in whatever direction, we see their bulk little by little increasing as if they were arising from the sea, whereas they seemed submerged because of the curvature of the earth's surface." Strabo, writing around AD 100, accepts the spherical shape of the earth as axiomatic, with north and south being its poles (*poloi*): "Let it be hypothesized that the earth together with the sea is *sphairoeidēs* (spherical)."

Four hundred years before Ptolemy, Eratosthenes had used the angles cast by the sun at the summer solstice to calculate the circumference of the earth at 252,000 stadia (28,970 miles), as Strabo tells us (*Geography* 2.5.7). Ptolemy is the first writer to articulate latitude. He does so using length of day at the summer solstice at a given point on the globe, which gets longer the further north one goes. Ptolemy even knows about the

Arctic Circle, the place where twenty-four-hour day and twenty-four-hour night each happen once a year.

Strabo is familiar with identifiable locations from Ïernē (Ireland) and Thulē (Norway) to Taprobanē (Sri Lanka, which he called the "Cinnamon-Producer") and Labadius (Java). He knows of the Golden (probably Malay) Peninsula, and the Great Gulf (Magnus Sinus). All of this belonged to what was called *India Trans Gangem* (India Across the Ganges). Long before Columbus, Strabo declares that "if the immensity of the Atlantic Ocean did not prevent it, we could sail from Iberia to India."

Ptolemy relies partly on information from Marinus of Tyre (early second century AD), and partly on the help of a Greek sailor named Alexander. Alexander tells that the eastern destination for Roman traders was a Burmese city called Tamala on the Malay Peninsula, where Eastern merchants then crossed to reach the Perimulic Gulf (Gulf of Thailand). He knows an important port city in the Far East called Cattigara, which has been identified close to Saigon, the former capital of South Vietnam. Ptolemy thinks that the two Latin names for China refer to different locations; to him, *Serica* (at the end of the Silk Road) is not the same place as *Sinae*, the land of the Qin dynasty. Ptolemy also knows Africa as far as the mountains of Mozambique, from where he says there are another seventy-four degrees to the Pole.

A first-century AD Greek text called the *Periplus of the Erythraean Sea* is another account of lands bordering the eastern Indian Ocean, written by an unnamed merchant. This writer also knows of a place that he pronounces *Thinae*, a great city where silk originates, in a land that stretches from the East all the way to the Caspian Sea. Even Josephus (*Antiquities* 8:164) knows enough about the Far East to theorize that the Golden Land (*Aurea Chersonesus*), which he says "belongs to India," is actually Ophir, the place from which Solomon and his Phoenician ships imported huge amounts of gold (1 Kings 10:11, 22).

So people in the first century AD biblical world were not locked in to the concept of a flat earth made up of Europe, northern Africa, and western Asia. Now, knowledge of the world was a bit sketchier when we go back a few centuries. The best maps we have for the ancient world from the Iron Age are the Sargon Geography map (eighth century BC, found in Wayne Horowitz, *Mesopotamian Cosmic Geography*), and—surprise!—the Table of Nations in Genesis 10. Kenneth Kitchen has demonstrated that Genesis

10 most likely reflects a tenth century BC date, based on the nations that appear and do not appear in it.[1]

So what was the Hebrew conception of the earth? The word *eretz* (used over 2500 times in the Hebrew Bible) was broad enough to mean "earth" as opposed to "sky/heaven" (Genesis 1:1), "land" in a more local sense (Genesis 12:1), "piece of property" (Genesis 23:15), or even "ground" in a directional sense (Genesis 18:2). However, the word *tēbēl* (used thirty-six times) is a narrower term, virtually always meaning "world" or "planet." Sometimes *eretz* and *tēbēl* are paired as poetic synonyms; sometimes they are glued together into a single expression (Job 37:12) to mean "the whole earth." Interestingly, the Greek version usually uses *oikoumenē* (inhabited world) to translate *tēbēl*, while Jerome, working around AD 400, uses the Latin *orbis*, which can mean either a circle or a sphere.

(By the way, *oikoumenē* is the word used where Jesus says that the Gospel must be preached to the entire world before he returns (Matthew 24:14 = Mark 13:10). The Gospel had already spread through the entire Roman Empire by the end of the first century AD, a possible fulfillment of Jesus' prediction, based on the meaning of *oikoumenē*. Whether or not Jesus meant every people group on the entire planet when he said the Gospel would be preached to the entire *oikoumenē*, I leave it to you as readers of God's word to decide for yourselves.)

The same Job who refers to the "pillars" of the earth in Job 9:6 (mentioned elsewhere only in Psalm 75:4, and in 1 Samuel 2:8, where a different word for pillar is used) also says in Job 26:7 that God "hangs the earth upon nothing." Neither description needs to be taken as an authoritative teaching on geology, especially not in a context from the mouth of Job. The "foundations of the earth" (mentioned only in 2 Samuel 22:16 = Psalm 18:16, and Isaiah 40:21) are less difficult to explain from our point of view than pillars; we may understand them as the "core" or mantle upon which the earth's crust rests.

Claims that the biblical writers believed in a flat earth tell us more about the people who make those dismissive claims than they do about the biblical writers themselves.

---

1. Kitchen, *Reliability of Old Testament*, 430–38.

14

Messiah's Mother: Virgin or Young Woman?

ʿALMAH IN ISAIAH 7:14—DOES this word mean "virgin" or merely "young woman"? Let's investigate. I think I can give you evidence far more extensive than the doubters will give you that this word really means "virgin."

"The virgin shall conceive." That's how the Greek Old Testament renders the verse in question. It uses the word *parthenos* (the standard word for "virgin") to translate the Hebrew term ʿ*almah*. The Jewish translators made this choice in their Greek version, almost three hundred years before Matthew seizes upon this line as a prophecy of the miraculous conception of Jesus.

After Matthew's use of the Septuagint to prove that the Messiah was prophesied to be virgin-born, Jews begin to backtrack from the rendering quoted by Matthew, from Aquila, Symmachus, and Theodotion (in their revised Greek translations), to Justin Martyr's fictional debate partner Trypho the Jew. Instead, they opt for the word *neanis* in their translations. And as time moves on to the so-called Enlightenment, we begin to hear that if Isaiah had meant "virgin," he would have used the word *betulah*, which is claimed to be unambiguous.

But wait a minute. First, *betulah* is no more unambiguous than ʿ*almah*. The Canaanite goddess Anath goes by the title "Virgin" (*btlt*), but her virginity is questionable (to the extent that one can question the factual details of a myth). Likewise, the virginity of Babylon (Isaiah 47:1) and even Israel are open to question, if collective identities can lose their virginity. True, *betulah* is most often accompanied by the specification that the girl has never had sexual experience, but one might ask whether that is necessary to spell out, if sexual inexperience is undoubtedly implied in the word. We also have strong reason to question the virginity of the *betulah* in Joel 1:8 (NRSV), where we read, "Lament like a virgin clothed in sackcloth for the husband of her youth."

Curiously, even the Greek *parthenos* is not as unambiguous as often thought. Dinah is still called a *parthenos* after she is violated by Shechem in Genesis 34:3 (translating the Hebrew *naʿarah*, "girl").

Second, we can dismiss the claim that the Hebrew term *ʿalmah* in Isaiah 7:14 can only mean "young woman." The word, in both its masculine and feminine forms, emphasizes the subject's youth and inexperience, such as when young David is called an *ʿelem* in 1 Samuel 17:56 (see also 1 Samuel 20:22, where *ʿelem* is used to describe what 20:35 calls a *naʿar qaton* or "little boy"). Miriam is called an *ʿalmah* in Exodus 2:8, and Proverbs 30:19 refers to the seduction of an *ʿalmah*, a verse which seems to imply that the girl has no prior sexual experience.

Where else is *ʿalmah* used? The five additional verses where this word is used in the Hebrew Bible add nothing pro or con to the debate about whether this word means "virgin." In Psalm 68:25, we have young girls playing tambourines, which is what the *ʿalamoth* in 1 Chronicles 15:20 and Psalm 46:1 may also be. In Song of Solomon 1:3, the girl sings to her beloved, "Therefore the young girls love you."

The only verse left that uses *ʿalmah* that has even a ghost of a chance of implying non-virginity is Song of Solomon 6:8, where the man compares his beloved to "sixty queens and eighty concubines, and maidens without number." Here, *ʿalmah* potentially becomes a victim of guilt by association with two other groups of women who are definitely not virgins. But again, what is proved? The *ʿalamoth* arguably becomes a category for the women for whom the male lead character has not had the leisure for carnal knowledge.

Finally, going back before Moses into the archaic Canaanite dialect of Hebrew known as Ugaritic, we find *ʿalmah* and *betulah* being used as poetic synonyms in a text cited by Ugaritic language pioneer Dr. Cyrus Gordon in his article "'*Almah* in Isaiah 7:14" (see bibliography). Gordon also gives us an example from Aramaic where *betultaʾ* is used to describe a pregnant woman who is have problems giving birth,[1] more proof that the *betulah* root is not guaranteed to always mean "virgin."

The ʿ*almah* root is also found in the substantive noun ʿ*alumīm*, "youth/youthfulness." which is found in Isaiah 54:4, Psalm 89:45, Job 20:11, and Job 33:25. Overall, the picture we get from this term ʿ*almah* is a picture of a girl who is young and inexperienced, a synonym of *naʿarah*, *betulah*, and *parthenos*.

So the claim that Isaiah 7:14's ʿ*almah* has no connotation of virginity is not as slam-dunk as we've been led to believe. Rather, ʿ*almah* is part of a semantic field of words that all emphasize youth and inexperience. The real question is how the birth of any child to any mother (virgin or not) seven hundred years in the future can be a sign to a king in Isaiah's day.

It appears that the initial sign to Ahaz was a normal birth that took place in the 730s BC. The supernatural conception and birth of Jesus of Nazareth seven hundred years in the future was Isaiah's prophecy "on steroids." It is the ultimate example of *sensus plenior*, a deeper sense put there by God that goes far beyond what the original human author would have grasped.

---

1. Gordon, *Ugaritic Textbook*, 377.

15

No Room for the Inn

It was not an "inn" where there was no room for Jesus' birth. The proof is in Mark 14:14 (= Luke 22:11), where Jesus books the same kind of place to eat the Last Supper. "Guest room" seems to be the best way to translate the Greek term *katalyma* used here and in Luke 2:7. The word *pandocheion*, used in Jesus' parable of the Good Samaritan (Luke 10), is the word for what we would understand as an inn. Since *katalyma* is only used three times in the New Testament, a look at the fourteen times *katalyma* is used in the Greek translation of the Hebrew Bible is in order.

In the Septuagint, the first time *katalyma* is used is in Exodus 4:24, where God meets Moses at a "lodging place" on the way back to Egypt and seeks to kill him; here, it likely means a camping place rather than a structure. Similarly, in 1 Samuel 1:18, Hannah and Eli are staying in a *katalyma* somewhere near the sanctuary in Shiloh, where they have come for an annual sacrifice (no word for lodging place is mentioned in the Hebrew text).

In 1 Samuel 9:22, *katalyma* appears to mean "banquet hall," as it does in Mark 14:14 = Luke 22:11; here, it is where Samuel hosts Saul and his servant for a meal, along with about thirty townspeople. In 1 Chronicles 28:13, the Greek adds a reference to *katalymata* to describe accommodations which Solomon builds for the priests who will serve in the Temple.

God's *katalyma* is first mentioned in Exodus 15:13, where it refers to God's holy "habitation," meaning either Sinai or possibly the Temple Mount, the place where God "lodges." Similarly, when God kindly declines David's offer to build him a house, God states that he has been living just fine in a *katalyma* and a tent (2 Samuel 7:6 = 1 Chronicles 17:5).

Out of the three times that *katalyma* is used in the Greek translation of Jeremiah, twice it refers to lodging places in the wilderness (14:8; 40:12), and once to a lion's lair (32:38). Ezekiel 23:21 criticizes Oholibah the nymphomaniac for letting the Egyptians handle her breasts "at your lodging place" (another place where the word *katalyma* is added where there is no corresponding word in the Hebrew). And later on during the rule of the Greek king Antiochus IV, we are told in 1 Maccabees 3:45 that "Jerusalem was uninhabited like a desert... The sanctuary was trampled down, and aliens were in the citadel; it was a *katalyma* for the Gentiles."

When Jesus is born in Bethlehem, Luke deliberately uses *katalyma* to describe the place where no room was to be found for the holy family. To stay in a *pandocheion* is out of the question, as argued by Ken Bailey in his online article "The Manger and the Inn" (see bibliography).

To give us an idea how bad the public inns were, Clement of Alexandria (*Stromateis* 2.20.114.5) quotes the second-century AD Gnostic Valentinus, who says the heart is like an inn, which also "has holes bored in it and dug in it and is often filled with *kopros* [dung] where people stay there and behave outrageously (*aselgōn*, a word for shocking sexual excess) with no consideration for the place, as if it were nothing to them."

The Jewish philosopher Philo uses the image of being "soiled and abused like someone entering a *pandocheion*." (*Questions and Answers on Genesis* 4:33) A lost fragment of Philo states that a *pandocheion* is a place where people "fill themselves and vomit in their passions." In the second-century AD Egerton Gospel Fragment line 8, a man says to Jesus, "While traveling and eating with lepers in the *pandocheion*, I myself also became a leper." (The barn is starting to sound better and better.)

Josephus (*Antiquities* 3:276) gives a list of the types of women a priest is forbidden to marry, including women who earned their living by innkeeping (*pandocheuein*), apparently because so much of the time their job involved practicing prostitution. Even worse, the rabbis declared that cattle cannot be trusted with Gentiles at an inn, because they practice bestiality (Mishnah, m. ʿ*Abodah Zarah* 2:1). An inscription listing prices at a Roman inn included wine and bread for one Roman *as* (one sixteenth of a denarius), *pulmentarium* (food to go with the bread) for two *asses*, hay for the mule for two *asses*, and a "girl" for eight *asses*.

Rabbinic Hebrew borrows the Greek term *pandocheion* in the form *pundaq*. In the Mishnah, the word is used in a case where a man dies at an inn on the road to the Dead Sea, possibly the very spot Jesus has in mind in his parable in Luke 10. The rabbis are looking for evidence to prove that the man died, so that the widow can remarry. The rabbis accept the lone testimony of the woman innkeeper, but they do so because she is able to present the man's staff, bag, and Torah scroll as evidence (m. *Yebamot* 16:7).

Yes, our Lord had a manger for a crib, but at least he wasn't born in a *pandocheion*. That would have been truly the bottom of the barrel.

16

Brothers or Cousins of Jesus?

ARE THE "BROTHERS" OF Jesus in Mark 6:3 really his cousins, or his half-brothers? Can the word "brother" (Greek *adelphos*, Hebrew *aḥ*) mean "cousin" in the Bible, and does the word "brother" mean "cousin" here in Mark's description of Jesus' nuclear family?

Protestants and Jews read Matthew's statement that Joseph and Mary had no sexual relations "until" (*eōs*) she gave birth to Jesus (Matthew 1:25) to strongly imply that they began a normal marital sex life after his birth. The fact that Mark names four brothers of Jesus and adds an unspecified number of sisters would support this understanding. The first-century Jewish historian Josephus also refers to James the Just as the "brother" of Jesus when describing James's execution by Jewish leaders in AD 62.

However, by the early second century, there developed a belief among some Christians that Mary remained a lifelong virgin. To explain Jesus' siblings, the early writer Epiphanius claimed that they were Joseph's children by a previous marriage. Certainly the word "brother" permits this possibility; neither Greek nor Hebrew provides for a distinction between "brother" and "step-brother" or the like. However, there is no convincing case for Joseph having been previously married, even though the *Protevangelium of James* (mid-second century AD) makes this claim.

Two voices in the early church firmly opposed the notion that Jesus was not blood-related to his reported siblings. One is the second-century AD writer Hegesippus, who refers to James as the "brother" of Jesus, while also mentioning an uncle and a cousin (*anepsion*) of Jesus. When he says "brother," he obviously does not mean generic relative. Hegesippus also refers to Jude as a brother of Jesus "according to the flesh."

The Latin writer Tertullian also insists that the brothers of Jesus were "true" (*vērē*) brothers. While Tertullian was a strong advocate of celibacy as being better than marriage, he firmly opposed the followers of Marcion and others who had Docetic views of Jesus' humanity. For Tertullian, the biological reality of Jesus' mother and brothers was part of his case against those who denied Jesus' true humanity.

What about the claim that the word "brothers" actually means "cousins" in Jesus' case? If this were true, it would incline us to believe not only that Mary remained a lifelong virgin, but that Joseph fathered no children with anyone. I see no reason whatsoever to believe that, but it wouldn't hurt to see if the word "brother" can be used in the Bible with the meaning of relatives outside one's nuclear family.

The answer is that it can, but only rarely. In Genesis 14:14 and 14:16, Abram's "brother" is his nephew Lot. In Genesis 31:37, 31:46, and 31:54, Jacob's "brothers" are his uncle Laban and his cousins. In Leviticus 10:4, the "brothers" of Nadab and Abihu (who die because they offered "strange fire" to YHWH) are their cousins.

But the word "brother" in biblical Hebrew can be, and does, get used even more broadly. In Exodus 2:11, Moses's "brothers" are his fellow Israelites. Throughout Deuteronomy, "brothers" means Israelites as opposed to foreigners. In Numbers 18:2 and 18:6, the word "brothers" means members of the same tribe. The term is also used broadly for extended family, such as the forty-two brothers of King Ahaziah who are killed by Jehu in 2 Kings 10:13, or the 130 brothers of Joel son of Gershom in 1 Chronicles 15:7, or the sixty-eight brothers of Obed-Edom in 1 Chronicles 16:38. (Granted, all these could be from prolific polygamous families, but they are more likely to mean extended family.)

Looked at in context, the brothers of Jesus are highly unlikely to have been anything other than the natural children of Joseph and Mary, to whom Jesus would have been a half-brother, if we accept (as I do) that Jesus was conceived without the help of Joseph or any human male (see chapter 14).

But here we do have a genuine royal blood line, so to speak—not the one touted by Dan Brown and others who believed that Jesus married and fathered a line of descendants (the Hebrew word for that is "hogwash!"), but a blood line descended from Joseph and Mary. The early church gave them the name *Desposynai* ("Those Belonging to the Master"). Their existence has been traced down to AD 313, when a delegation of them goes to Pope Sylvester and asks to be reinstated as leaders of the Jerusalem church (a request which was denied).

Wouldn't it be cool if we knew someone who was a direct descendant of Joseph and Mary? Perhaps. But Jesus himself minimizes the significance of blood relationship to him during his earthly life, when his mother and brothers come to visit him on the road in Mark 3:31–35. What does Jesus say? "Whoever does the will of God, this is my brother and sister and mother."

17

Christ the Builder?

WAS JESUS A CARPENTER, or a builder? Was he actually a construction worker?

Jesus' father Joseph is commonly identified as being a "carpenter," a word that implies that Jesus and his father worked with wood for a career. The term *tektōn* is found only twice in the New Testament, in a doubly attested quote where Jesus is referred to as either "the carpenter" (Mark 6:3) or "the son of the carpenter" (Matthew 13:55). Further investigation, however, will show that *tektōn* is a generic word for "builder," in the same sense that *architektōn* (= "architect") means "chief builder" (1 Corinthians 3:10).

The Liddell-Scott lexicon of ancient Greek states that the use of *tektōn* to mean anything other than "carpenter" is relatively rare. But the Greek Old Testament (where *tektōn* is used thirty times) is a treasure trove of examples of *tektōn* being used in such ways. The Greek version often differentiates between a crafter "of wood," a crafter "of stone," or a crafter "of iron." So in 1 Samuel 13:19, a "*tektōn* of iron" is a "blacksmith" (see also Isaiah 44:12). And in 2 Samuel 5:11, the "carpenters and masons" sent to David by King Hiram are "*tektonas* of wood" and "*tektonas* of stone," while in 1 Kings 7:14, a half-Tyrian artisan named Hiram hired by Solomon is a "*tektōn* of bronze."

But in some passages, the *tektones* are distinguished from the "stonecutters" (*latomoi*—Ezra 3:7) and/or the "builders" (*oikodomoi*—2 Chronicles 34:11). However, in each of these examples, there are specific Hebrew terms that explain the use of different Greek terms; the Hebrew *ḥarash* (generic "craftsman") is consistently translated by *tektōn* in the Greek, as seen in 2 Chronicles 34:11. Indeed, in Ezra 3:7, both words are translated into Latin as *cementarius* (a worker in cement, a mason).

Hosea 8:6 says of the golden calf in Samaria, "A *tektōn* made it; it is not God." If this idol was solid metal rather than a gold-plated wood carving, then a *tektōn* does not necessarily work with a saw, hammer, and nails. Hosea 13:2 also speaks of those who construct molten images of silver as *tektones*. Likewise, Isaiah 40:19 speaks of a *tektōn* "casting" or "pouring" a molten idol, while in the very next verse a *tektōn* is crafting an idol of wood.

Josephus uses the plural of *tektōn* to refer to those who constructed Moses's tabernacle (*Antiquities* 3:204). In his descriptions of the construction of Solomon's and Herod's temples, like the accounts in Kings and Chronicles, Josephus distinguishes between stonecutters and *tektonas*, with no indication whether the *tektones* are involved in the stone-laying process, or are only involved in woodwork. In *Jewish War* 3:78, Josephus calls the men who construct the Roman military camps *tektones*. And in *Jewish War* 3:171, Josephus tells that he ordered his *tektonas* to build a (presumably) stone fortification wall higher in order to defend his city (3:173 and 5:275 also refer to them building city walls).

Do these uses of *tektōn* throw more light on what Jesus and his earthly father did for a living? They certainly broaden the possibilities. They tell us that Jesus had muscle and technical skill. If not for the fact that Joseph and Mary offer the lowest-price option for their Temple sacrifice when Jesus is born, we might think that their family belonged to the upper middle class.

Later on, near the end of the first century AD, according to the historian Eusebius, Jesus' nephews appear before the emperor Domitian, who is afraid that because these Christian leaders are descendants of David, they may try to rebel and set up their own kingdom. When he examines their hands, however, and see that they are rough from manual labor, and that these men had only a modest amount of land, he released them as being no danger to the empire. This is the only other clue we have that Jesus and his family could be classified as "blue collar."

We may compare Jesus' pre-ministry career with the professions held by other rabbis in Jesus' day. We are told that Shammai was also a carpenter. Hillel was a day laborer. Others were shoemakers, shopkeepers, and professional writers. Saul of Tarsus was a tentmaker. But it does not appear that Jesus practiced his profession once he left Nazareth to proclaim God's word; he appears to have relied on the hospitality of those who wished to benefit from his ministry. Luke 8:1–3 names some women of wealth who followed him and provided for him. This is not out of line with the practice of the above-named rabbis, who often could not earn enough by part-time labor to keep themselves out of poverty, and who survived only because of the additional generosity of others.

It is because the term *tektōn* is better translated "builder" rather than "carpenter" that I have rewritten the children's TV theme song "Bob the Builder" and re-titled it "Christ the Builder." Followers of Christ: hard hat, anyone?

18

Same-Sex Intimacy: What Does Jesus Say?

How many times have we heard that claim that "Jesus never spoke one word on homosexual behavior"? I would argue that yes, he did. We find that word on his list of sins that defile the human heart in Mark 7:21–23, where Jesus names not only adultery and heterosexual sex outside of marriage, but also the sin of *aselgeia*.

Aselgeia is a term that is usually translated "lewdness," "licentiousness," or "lasciviousness," but it appears to be the Greek word used by first century Jews to refer to sexual behavior that goes beyond mere fornication or adultery.

Before I go any further, you may wonder, "Is Jesus anti-gay?" That's a very different question than to ask, "Does Jesus think sex is OK between members of the same sex?" If we presume that Jesus hates all people who do stuff that he names on this sin list, then Jesus must hate everybody! No, that's the wrong way to read Jesus' teaching. *Jesus is not labeling same-sex attraction as sin.* The issue is not our desires, but how we handle those desires.

I have made the argument that *aselgeia* is Jesus' veiled term for homosexual behavior and other similar sexual offenses forbidden in the Torah in my journal article "*Aselgeia* in Mark 7:22." You can find the link to the scholar's version at www.biblicalethic.org. The layperson's version may be found in Appendix Two of my book *What's on God's Sin List for Today?*

The basic meaning of this word in Greek is shocking behavior that goes way over the line. It can include outrageous insults. Plutarch uses the word for men who deliberately vomited at dinner and pooped on their chairs, while Demosthenes uses it for men who dumped chamberpots on their host. But the word is more often used for shocking sexual behavior, including a man who has sex with his slave in public at a party, a Roman soldier who waves his penis at a crowd in Jerusalem, and "a single young man who through *aselgeia* has become the lover of an entire city" (Heraclitus, Epistle 7.5). In the *Testaments of the Twelve Patriarchs*, Jews use the word for not only unrestrained fornication, but also incest, pederasty, and bestiality.

The word *aselgeia* is used ten times in the New Testament. Second Peter, which uses the word three times (2:2, 2:7, 2:18), links it clearly to the sin of Sodom. Jude 1:4 describes those "who twist the grace of our God into *aselgeia*." The word appears in Paul's famous list of the works of the flesh in Galatians 5:19. It also tops the list of objectionable pagan behaviors in 1 Peter 4:3. In Ephesians 4:19, Paul says that pagans "have given themselves up to *aselgeia*, greedy to practice every kind of uncleanness." (See also Romans 13:13 and 2 Corinthians 12:21.) The word is never used in any book where Paul's specific word for homosexual, *arsenokoitēs* (1 Corinthians 6:9, 1 Timothy 1:10), is used.

Outside of the New Testament, *aselgeia* often occurs in a standard trio of sexual vices alongside fornication and adultery, in the same spot in the trio often occupied by *arsenokoitēs* or *paiderastia* (molestation of boys). An example is Melito's sermon *On the Passover*, where *aselgeia* is used in the trio of vices, and then the speaker describes as the ultimate degree of *aselgeia* cases where "father cohabits with his child, and son with his mother, and brother with sister, and male with male, and each man neighing after the wife of his neighbor."

How did the earliest Christians translate this word? Syriac is the closest language to Aramaic, the language that Jesus spoke. Our Syriac versions use a word that means licentiousness or lewdness. This Syriac word comes from an Aramaic word that conveys a terrible stench. The specific Aramaic word that Jesus probably used never appears in print, which leads me to wonder whether it was unprintable (!) due to Jewish reluctance to talk about the subject unless absolutely necessary.

According to both the *Oxford Latin Dictionary* and Craig Williams, author of *Roman Homosexuality*, the translation of this word used in the Old Latin versions, *impudicitia*, points strongly to homosexual behavior in men. Suetonius says about Julius Caesar (*Julius* 52.3), "Lest there be any doubt in anyone's mind that he was notorious indeed both for his *impudicitia* and his adulteries, the elder Curio called him in one of his speeches 'every woman's man and every man's woman.'" It is this sense of *impudicitia* that is arguably the meaning behind Mark's use of *aselgeia* in transmitting the words of Jesus in Mark 7:22.

The likelihood that *aselgeia* is Jesus' term for homosexual behavior is strengthened by his clear overarching teaching on marriage in Matthew 19:1–6 (= Mark 10:1–9). As I wrote in my Patheos post, "God's Sex Mandate: The Two Shall Become One Flesh," Genesis, Jesus, and Paul all teach God's central teaching on sex: it belongs only in a lifelong one-flesh relationship between a man and a woman. Jesus only endorses celibacy and committed heterosexual marriage. And Jesus was enough of a non-conformist that if he had believed in same-sex relationships, he would have said so.

Does this sin list in Mark really comes from Jesus, or did the early church make it up? Jesus scholar John Meier believes that the list reads like a catechism for Gentiles who need the basics of morality spelled out for them. I would counter that every rabbi had his own *halakah* (code of conduct) for his followers; here, we have Jesus' *halakah*, given right when he has just set aside the kosher food laws. And despite Meier's skepticism about whether Jesus spoke these actual words, Meier writes in volume 3 of his book *A Marginal Jew: Rethinking the Historical Jesus*:

> On *sexual* matters, Jesus and the Essenes tend in the same direction: stringent standards and prohibitions . . . In a sense, one could call both Jesus and the Essenes extreme conservatives . . . apart from the two special cases of divorce and celibacy, where he diverged from mainstream Judaism, his views *were* those of mainstream Judaism. Hence there was no pressing need for him to issue or for the earliest Christian Jews to enshrine moral pronouncements about matters on which all Law-abiding Jews agreed.[1]

Underneath the reality of same-sex desire is the God-given need all of us have for love and affirmation from our own gender. The road to healing seems to lie in meeting that need in non-sexual ways. Christians need to be the ones God uses to extend that kind of love to those who experience same-sex desire. That's the heart I see behind what Jesus says: to set us free from anything that harms us. That's the ultimate purpose in Jesus' list of warnings of what throws the human heart off track. Mark gives us a tantalizing one-word clue as to what Jesus thinks on this subject.

---

1. Meier, *Marginal Jew* 3, 502–3.

19

Eunuchs in Biblical Times

Eunuchs have unfortunately become another attempted biblical argument in favor of rewriting the Bible's sexual ethic. The argument has been around for years, based on the story of the Ethiopian eunuch who comes to Christ in Acts 8:26–39.

It is sad to hear a passage that celebrates the first messenger of the Gospel to Africa, turned into a claim that the story was all about the sexual status of the Ethiopian official. Since this passage has played a key role in convincing quite a few scholars to change their minds on homosexuality, this passage merits further discussion.

The Hebrew word *sarīs* can mean both "royal official" and "eunuch." The word is used of Potiphar, Joseph's Egyptian master in Genesis 39. Despite the fact that Potiphar's wife appears there as a sex-starved "Desperate Housewife," we have no reason to believe that her husband had been rendered incapable of normal marital relations.

The Hebrew term in question comes from Akkadian, the language of the Assyrians and Babylonians, where it may be seen even in the title Rab-Saris (chief official) in 2 Kings 18:17 and Jeremiah 39:3. There is no hint of emasculation in the term, but large numbers of royal servants were subjected to this procedure, although this is less likely in the few examples of *sarīsīm* cited in Israel (1 Samuel 8:15, 1 Kings 22:9, 2 Kings 24:15, and Ebed-Melech the Ethiopian in Jeremiah 38:7). Daniel and his three friends may have been emasculated as a condition of their service to the Babylonian king.

It is true that as a literal *eunuchos*, the Ethiopian official in Acts 8 would not have been able to go any further into the Temple than the Court of the Gentiles. However, unless he had converted to Judaism, he would not have been able to enter any further than that point, anyway. And the Mishnah (m. *Yebamot* 8:1) states that if a priest has suffered the injury or loss of his genitals, he is still allowed to eat the holy offerings; he simply is not allowed to enter "the Assembly" (it is unclear whether this means only the Temple, or may also apply to the local synagogue).

The rabbis in the Mishnah (first two centuries AD) do not make eunuchs out to be evil people, and actually say very little about them. They make much less of an issue out of the eunuch's sexual status than today's defenders of the gay agenda, who wish to overstate the evidence by making the eunuch into a symbol for those who practice same-gender sexual intimacy.

Even though eunuchs were emasculated to prevent misconduct with women, they were still often stigmatized as immoral because of the belief that they were sexually active with their own gender. That is precisely why Deuteronomy 23:1 keeps them out of the sanctuary: because the vast majority of eunuchs in the Late Bronze Age and Iron Age I were made, not for government service, but for cultic male prostitution. The Mosaic prohibition no doubt was more sweeping than necessary, but is comparable to today's sweeping prohibitions on who can donate blood. Who can enter God's sanctuary was just as serious an issue.

So, is this a case where God commands a change in his own law? I would argue that God already announced such a change in Isaiah 56:4–5. God doesn't explicitly say, "OK, you can come into the Temple now," but God declares in this passage that eunuchs who keep the Sabbath and "choose the things that please me and hold fast my covenant" will receive "in my house and within my walls a monument and a name better than sons and daughters." They will receive "an everlasting name that shall not be cut off" (NRSV).

As I have argued in my book *What's on God's Sin List for Today?*, when God reaffirms an Old Testament command in the New Testament, and/or places a death penalty on the offense, these are signs that this is a moral principle that is timeless and universal. Deuteronomy 23:1 meets neither of these criteria. In fact, Acts 8:26–39 is there to explicitly reverse God's previous command. When the eunuch asks, "Is there anything that prevents me from being baptized?", the answer is, "Nothing!" By contrast, homosexual behavior both carries a death penalty and is reaffirmed on the New Testament sin lists in 1 Corinthians 6:9–11, 1 Timothy 1:9–11, and arguably on Jesus' sin list in Mark 7:21–23 under the term *aselgeia*, translated as "licentiousness" (see chapter 18, and my article "*Aselgeia* in Mark 7:22" in the bibliography).

There are no legitimate grounds for equating the issue of being a eunuch with the issue of same-gender sexual activity. For Jesus in Matthew 19:10–12, being a eunuch means nothing more or less than sexual abstinence (for both genders, presumably, based on how Jesus makes his argument in this passage). Jesus says that some abstain because they were born without the means to participate in sexual intercourse, some were artificially deprived of that ability, and some choose not to participate for reasons related to their devotion to God.

Jesus in effect agrees with the words of his disciples that it may be better not to marry at all. How does that fit with God's words in the Garden, "It is not good for the human to be alone"? The bottom line is that Jesus affirms both: sexual abstinence, and lifelong faithful marriage between a man and a woman. But Jesus neither blesses nor endorses any third option.

Acts 8:26–39 is a wonderful account of an African royal treasurer who takes several months off from his job to travel nine hundred miles to seek the God of Israel. He even purchases an expensive personal copy of the Septuagint. Here is a man who fulfills Isaiah's 700-year-old prophecy that worshippers will come to Jerusalem "from beyond the rivers of Sudan . . . from a nation tall and smooth . . . whose land the rivers divide" (Isaiah 18:1–7). This man becomes the firstfruits of the Gospel in Africa. Let's leave the account the way that Luke intended it to be read.

20

Concubine Versus Married Woman in the Bible

WHAT IS A "CONCUBINE" in the Bible? We know she's not a wife, but what exactly is she? What constitutes "marriage?" And how do we classify all of the other sexual activity outside of marriage in the biblical world?

The word *pilegesh* (a non-Semitic word, possibly related to Greek *pallakis*) is used thirty-seven times in the Hebrew Bible. Eleven of these are in the story of the live-in girl whom the Levite in Judges 19 never bothered to marry. No wife is ever mentioned for this guy, and he surrenders the girl to the mob in Gibeah. Yet the girl's father is called the Levite's "father-in-law" (*ḥotam*) in Judges 19:7. And when she runs away in 19:2 to return to her father's house (a rarely if ever attested phenomenon in biblical narrative), she is said to have "played the harlot" against her partner—a most peculiar halfway relationship that reveals what a mess Israel has become in the time of the judges.

Other concubines worthy of note are David's ten concubines whom his son Absalom takes for himself (2 Samuel 15:16, 16:21–22), Abimelech's mother (Judges 8:31), Saul's concubine Rizpah (2 Samuel 3:7—notice that he has only one), Solomon's three hundred concubines, Rehoboam's sixty concubines (2 Chronicles 11:21), and the concubines of Ahasuerus in Esther. Belshazzar's concubines in Daniel 5:2 are *shegalat* or "paramours" (to put it nicely). Otherwise, concubines in the Hebrew Bible are surprisingly few.

Bilhah, one of two maids by whom Jacob has children, is called a concubine (Genesis 35:22), and Abraham is said in Genesis 25:6 to have had concubines, presumably Keturah and Hagar, although Keturah is also called a "wife" in 25:1. (There is no unambiguous Hebrew word for "wife." The standard term, *ishshah*, is also the standard word for "woman," so only context can tell us when it means "wife." The other term is *beʿulah*, as in the Gospel hymn "Beulah Land," literally "belonging to a *baʿal*/master," an unflattering way to refer to a wife.)

The one place where a *woman* is said to have had "concubines" (*pilegeshīm*) is Ezekiel 23:20, that infamous verse where the nymphomaniac girl Oholibah (Judah) is said to have lusted after her "paramours." Herein seems to be a clue to the overarching meaning of the word: a steady sex partner without the legal status or protections of marriage. Some concubines, like Bilhah, were acquired by purchase or inheritance. In royal harems, such as in Esther, they were wives other than the queen. But concubines never fit God's standard, "The two shall become one flesh" (Genesis 2:24).

Near Eastern law from before the time of Moses declares, "If a man takes a wife but does not establish her contract, that woman is not a wife" (Law of Hammurabi 128) . We may ask: What's in a clay tablet? Or why is a modern "piece of paper" so important? Answer: Who would put $50,000 down on a house without a legal document testifying that the house now belongs to you? In the biblical world, the contract makes all the difference.

The same Near Eastern law tradition also provides for the status of a secondary wife, called a *šugītu* in Babylonian. It is unclear whether a *šugītu* is the equivalent of a *pilegesh* (concubine); if so, her secondary status would be clearly stated in the husband's contract with both women. However, we have no evidence that the Hebrew *pilegesh* had any written contract or protections.

In the New Testament, other than the woman at the well in John 4, concubines or live-in sex partners are absent entirely. The Greek *pallakē* (= *pallakis*) is only found in the Septuagint and in non-biblical Greek. Josephus tells us twice that the children of a *pallakē* are *nothoi*, that is, not legitimate (*Antiquities* 2:5, 5:233). We find this same understanding in the Greek orator Demosthenes's famous line, "Courtesans we have for the sake of pleasure, concubines for the daily care of the body, wives for having children legitimately" (*Against Nearea* 59.122).

In Hebrew thought, all other sex outside of marriage is harlotry, *za-nuth*, whether paid or unpaid. Harlotry was a tolerated (but *not* approved) option, but only for emancipated women. There was no swinging singles scene in Late Bronze/Iron Age Israel. Premarital sex was rectified by either enforced marriage or by payment equal to what the guy would have paid to marry a virgin (Exodus 22:16–17). And the New Testament clearly teaches that *porneia* (= *zanuth* = fornication) is clearly on God's sin list (see Mark 7:21, 1 Corinthians 5:11 and 6:9, Galatians 5:19, Ephesians 5:3, Colossians 3:5, 1 Thessalonians 4:3, Revelation 22:15).

So what makes a marriage in biblical times, then? The Bible specifies no marriage ceremony. Isaac appears to simply take Rebecca into his mother's tent, although a contract is probably assumed. And Ruth proposes to Boaz in a most unusual encounter that even Boaz disavows as a norm to be followed. But the Hebrew Bible speaks of marriage as a covenant (*berīth*), an iron-clad promise (Proverbs 2:17, Ezekiel 16:8, Malachi 2:14).

The rabbis taught in the Mishnah that a woman could be betrothed by either money, a written betrothal, or by intercourse (m. *Qiddušin* 1:1). But the third option was impractical, because it required witnesses to the couple being alone together who hear the man say, "You are betrothed to me by this intercourse." Even in this case, however, the resulting betrothal becomes as binding as a marriage, and can be broken only by divorce, as we see in the case of Joseph deciding how to divorce Mary quietly before marriage (Matthew 1:19).

What was marriage, then? The couple lived apart before the wedding. The wedding was the night when the couple finally moves in together, after the groom concludes the final details of the contract with the bride's family. The Parable of the Ten Virgins (Matthew 25) and the wedding at Cana (John 2) are the only pictures we have of a biblical wedding, and neither of them gives us the "how to" details we want to know.

It takes more than the vows of a couple and the pronouncement of God's representative to make a marriage. But these are where it starts. Without these, we can easily fool ourselves into pursuing levels of intimacy that we should never pursue, with partners to whom we should never be joined. An article by Judith Krantz in *Cosmopolitan* magazine called "Living Together Is a Rotten Idea" (see bibliography) makes a non-religious case against cohabitation that is still valid and convincing today.

Life as a concubine looks like a rip-off. Marriage matters, tremendously. If we are looking for a romantic relationship, we are wise not to settle for less than God's best.

21

Desire, Lust, and Coveting: It's All the Same Word!

DESIRE CAN BE GOOD, bad, or neither. In the New Testament, it's all the same word. Lust, coveting, everyday neutral desires, and even holy desires are all covered by the same Greek noun (*epithymia*) and related verb (*epithymeō*). To use any one of these English terms (lust, coveting, desire, longing) is a value judgment we must make as we translate God's word. When we find the word "lust" in our Bible (usually meaning a sexual desire, usually with negative overtones), underneath it is a word that could just as easily refer to a non-sexual, totally innocent desire in a different context.

Lent is a good time to take a look at the subject of desire. When we think of Lent, we think of resisting desires that are not good for us, but the Bible's word in question covers all sorts of desires, including good ones.

For instance, at the Last Supper, Jesus literally says, "I have desired with desire to eat this Passover with you before I suffer" (Luke 22:15). Here this word obviously does not mean "lust," but a much different kind of desire. In 1 Timothy 3:1, Paul writes, "If anyone aspires to be an *episkopēs* (overseer or "bishop"), he desires a good work." Again, this sounds like a positive desire, not a decadent one. In Philippians 1:23, Paul says he has a "desire" to depart this life and be with Christ, a holy desire!

In Matthew 13:17, Jesus tells his followers, "Many prophets and righteous people desired/longed to see what you see, and did not see it, and to hear what you hear, but did not hear it"—here, the object of that desire is Jesus' life and words themselves (angels have that same "desire" in 1 Peter

1:12). The Greek Old Testament speaks of *"longing* for your judgment" (Psalm 119:20) and says, "I *long* for your precepts" (Psalm 119:40). Even the Holy Spirit has holy "desires" that are opposed to what the flesh wants (Galatians 5:17).

Don't assume that the "lusts" or "desires" mentioned in the Bible are necessarily sexual. In 1 John 2:16, John speaks of two kinds of desire: the "lusts of the flesh" (the desire for pleasure) and "the lust of the eyes" (= coveting, the desire to acquire). In Mark 4:19, Jesus teaches that the "desires for other (unspecified) things" choke God's word in our hearts. In Romans 6:12, Paul writes, "Do not let sin reign in your mortal body, in order to obey its (unspecified) desires." In James 1:15, we see that "desire" (unspecified) gives birth to sin. In 2 Timothy 4:3, we are told that in the last days, people will accumulate teachers according to their own "desires" to hear what they want to hear.

One kind of "desire" covered by the word *epithymia* is for food. In Luke 15:16, the Prodigal Son "longs" (lusts?) to gorge himself with the dry carob pods that he is feeding to the pigs. Similarly, Lazarus "longs" to be fed from the crumbs from the rich man's table in Luke 16:21.

Another desire covered by this word is the desire for material possessions. The verb *epithymeō* is the verb used in the tenth commandment, "Thou shalt not covet," and is the standard Greek term for "coveting." In 1 Timothy 6:9, Paul warns believers against getting hooked into "desires" for money and other treasures that are not evil in themselves, but which can easily plunge people into ruin and misery in their efforts to acquire them.

And yes, *epithymia* also is used for sexual desire, where it can be translated "lust." In 1 Thessalonians 4:5, Paul urges believers that they should marry in holiness and honor, "not in the passion of desire, like heathen who do not know God." Marriage that is based on physical desire alone is on shaky ground. And Jesus puts the moral bar sky-high when he teaches in Matthew 5:28 that anyone who looks at a person "in order to desire" him/her has already committed adultery in his/her heart.

We may ask, What's the difference between "lust" and mere attraction? Aren't they both forms of desire, distinguished only by degree? Yes they are, which is why it is fitting that God's word employs a term for these that is equally ambiguous. "Desire" is good. It becomes bad only when we let it drag us into wanting what we should not have. God put within us the longing for a mate, but God also intended that desire to be channeled into a relationship with one person, a context where we can enjoy the maximum happiness of a lifelong one-flesh union (see my Patheos post, "God's Sex Mandate: The Two Shall Become One Flesh").

It is sad that even our most innocent human desires tend to become a bottomless pit. In *Memorabilia* 2.1.30, the Greek writer Xenophon paints a picture of pleasure as a vice that could just as easily describe desire: "O Wretch, what moral good do you know, or what good do you perceive with your senses? One who does not even wait for the appetite (*epithymia*) for pleasant foods, eating before hunger, drinking before thirst; and so that you may eat pleasantly, seeking out skillful cooks; and so that you may drink pleasantly, procuring expensive wines; and who in summer runs about seeking snow; and so that you may sleep pleasantly, not only provides soft beds, but also supports to the couches."

In God's new creation, we look forward to the resolving of every good desire. No more "I want" in heaven. But it won't be a place full of "goodies on steroids." What we wanted down here, was only a poor substitute for the true joys for which our hearts have longed. Let's get a grip on that glorious truth, particularly in the season of Lent.

22

Belial and Sons

OUR BOSS IS "SUCH a son of *beliyyaʿal* [the equivalent of English "S.O.B."] that one cannot speak to him." Thus say the ranch-hands at Nabal's ranch in 1 Samuel 25:17. Our Bibles obscure the presence of the Hebrew term *beliyyaʿal* in this verse. Instead, they say that Nabal is "so ill-natured" (NRSV) or "such a scoundrel" (NKJV). But "S.O.B." would be a fitting (albeit hybrid) abbreviation of this expression "Son Of Belial." Poor guy—even his wife Abigail calls him an "S.O.B." in 1 Samuel 25:25!

We look in vain for the word *beliyyaʿal* in any other Semitic language that I know of. It is actually a combination of a poetic word for "not" plus the word "profitable," giving us the meaning "worthless(ness)" or "good-for-nothing." All but five of its twenty-seven occurrences in the Hebrew Bible refer to people. It also refers to a wicked thought in Deuteronomy 15:9, and to a deadly disease in Psalm 41:8. The writer of Psalm 101:3 declares, "I will not set before my eyes anything that is base/wicked." And in 2 Samuel 22:5 (= Psalm 18:5), *beliyyaʿal* is personified as an evil power paired with Death that is poised to gang up on David.

It's interesting to look at who all is called a son (or man) of *beliyyaʿal* in the Bible, an expression usually translated as "worthless men" or "scoundrels." We begin the list with the lone example of the expression "daughter of *beliyyaʿal*," which Hannah begs Eli the priest not to think that she is one, when he mistakes her for a drunken woman (1 Samuel 1:16).

The men in Deuteronomy 13:13, who would lead an entire town astray to worship idols, are called "sons of *beliyyaʿal*." So are the men of Gibeah who demanded sex from the traveling Levite (Judges 19:22, 20:13). So are the sons of Eli (1 Samuel 2:12), who treated the sanctuary offerings with contempt, and slept with the women who served at the sanctuary. So are the men who questioned Saul's appointment as king (1 Samuel 10:27), and the men who refused to share the Amalekite plunder with the men who stayed behind with the baggage (1 Samuel 30:22).

Shimei calls David a man of *beliyyaʿal* while throwing rocks and dust at him in 2 Samuel 16:7. Sheba son of Bichri, who seeks to lead another rebellion against David, is also called this name in 2 Samuel 20:1. Two "S.O.B.'s" are recruited as false witnesses to accuse Naboth and put him to death (1 Kings 21:10, 13). And Abijah is quoted as saying that it was "S.O.B.'s" who pressured Rehoboam into making a bad decision that lost him the kingdom (2 Chronicles 13:7).

Nahum is the only prophet to use the term *beliyyaʿal* (1:11 and 1:15). He uses it to refer to a "counselor," who is probably the king of Nineveh, who plots evil and destruction against all surrounding nations, and even the Lord himself. Judah is promised that never more shall Belial pass through her, at least, not in an Assyrian uniform. In the book of Nahum, *Beliyya'al* is beginning to transform from an unflattering adjective into a character larger than life.

When we get to the New Testament period, the personification of *beliyyaʿal* as an evil power, which we found only in 2 Samuel 22:5 = Psalm 18:5, becomes a standard name for Satan, a function it almost never serves in the Hebrew Bible. Paul writes in 2 Corinthians 6:15, in a passage that juxtaposes light with darkness and the temple of God with idols, "What agreement does Christ have with Beliar?" (The spelling Beliar is used when the name occurs in Greek.) Here Belial is clearly another name for Satan.

Belial is also mentioned in at least two different sections of the Dead Sea Scrolls. He is named eleven times in the War Scroll (1QM). He is also mentioned four times in "The Coming of Melchizedek" (11Q13), where he is named among the spirits who have rebelled against God and have become utterly wicked; Melchizedek "will deliver all the captives from the power of Belial."

In chapter 4 of the book *The Martyrdom and Ascension of Isaiah*, we hear that "Beliar, the great angel and king of this world . . . will descend from his firmament in the form of a man, a king of iniquity, a murderer of his mother" (sounds like a reappearance of Nero). It says he will claim to be God and will speak and act like the Beloved, and all will believe in him;

many of the saints will be led astray. He is to raise the dead and perform many signs, like making the sun rise at midnight. He will rule for three years, seven months, and twenty-seven days, he will set up his image in every city, and do whatever he wishes. And at the end of his rule, the Lord will come "and will drag Beliar, and his hosts also, into Gehenna." After this revelation, in 5:1, Beliar incites Manasseh to saw Isaiah in two.

The Sibylline Oracles also present Nero in a similar way: "Then Beliar will come from the line of Augustus . . . and he will raise up the dead and perform many signs for men . . . And he will lead astray many faithful, chosen Hebrews." In the end, God sends fire to burn up Beliar and his followers (Sibylline Oracles 3.63–74).

In other Jewish writings in Greek, Beliar is also found twice in Jubilees (1:20, 15:33), four times in Lives of the Prophets, and eleven times in the Testaments of the Twelve Patriarchs. In Testament of Reuben 6:3, women are "the plague of Beliar." Testament of Levi 18:12 says that "Beliar shall be bound by him" (by a new priest, possibly the Messiah?). Testament of Dan 5:10 says that the Lord "will make war against Beliar." And Testament of Judah 25:3 says that "Beliar's spirit of error shall be no more, because he will be thrown into eternal fire."

It would certainly appear that Satan is the great "Son Of Belial"—if it were not for the fact that he is the spiritual father of them all!

23

Killing, Smiting, and Other Casualties

THERE'S A HUGE DIFFERENCE between being killed or wounded. But that difference is not always clear in the language used in the Bible, particularly when the word "smite" is used.

We have that problem in today's world also. When reading about a battle from the American Civil War, or about recent military clashes, the casualty reports can be confusing if not misleading to people like me. We hear that there were 120 casualties, but then we find out that actually means that there were twenty soldiers killed and one hundred wounded.

The verb *hikkah* (used five hundred times in the Hebrew Bible) is just as misleading as the English noun "casualty." *Hikkah* can mean either "smite" or "kill" (it is usually translated by the Greek *patassō* or the Latin *percussit*), and often it is unclear and debatable as to which meaning we should prefer. And the difference is too important to simply leave it to our Bible translation. Did the Philistines die when they were smitten, or not? Was the particular attack fatal, or merely debilitating? Even if you have never studied Hebrew, a copy of Strong's or Young's concordance can tell you whether the word in question in the passage you are reading is *hikkah* or another word. Let's take a look at some examples, many of which should be familiar.

When Jonathan "smote" the Philistine garrison at Geba (1 Samuel 13:3), it is better to translate "attacked" or "defeated" than to think that Jonathan killed them all. Genesis 32:9, Joshua 11:8 ("smote *and* chased"), and Judges 3:13 are all examples where "attacked" is the best way to translate. But 1 Samuel 17:50 makes it clear that David both "smote" Goliath and "put him to death," two separate actions. In 1 Samuel 17:35, David smites the lion or bear to rescue his sheep, and if the animal attacks him, he smites *and* kills it. In Exodus 2:11, Moses sees an Egyptian boss "beating" a Hebrew slave but not killing him (same meaning in 2:13 and in 5:14), but in the very next verse, Moses "smote" the Egyptian and hid him in the sand (verse 14 confirms that this blow was fatal).

In 1 Kings 22:24, a false prophet "smote" the prophet Micaiah on the cheek, but he does not die. Likewise, the angel "smote" the men of Sodom with blindness, but they do not die (Genesis 19:11). Job 2:7 states that Satan smites Job with bad sores, not with death. The princes smite Jeremiah (Jeremiah 37:15), but he does not die. Psalm 121:6 promises, "The sun shall not smite you by day, nor the moon by night." On disciplining a child, Proverbs 23:13 says, "If you beat him with a rod, he will not die." (Ask Moses's victim about that!) Deuteronomy 25:2 is the only law that prescribes "beating" (*not* execution) as a punishment. But God "smites" the firstborn in Egypt (Exodus 12:29), and they die. Phineas smites the Israelite and his Midianite sex partner with a spear, and they both die (Numbers 25:14–15).

The difference becomes all the more important in historical and legal passages where the context does not make the meaning clear. Samson "smote" a thousand men with the jawbone of a donkey (Judges 15:15)—did they all die? Even Samson's line "heaps upon heaps" does not rule out survivors in the pile. But there is no clue as to how many died when Shamgar "smote" six hundred men with an ox goad (Judges 3:31). And what do the ladies mean in 1 Samuel 18:7 when they sing, "Saul has smitten his thousands"? When God smites seventy men who peeked inside the Ark of the Covenant in 1 Samuel 6:19, did they all die? In 1 Kings 20:29, Israel smites 100,000 in one day, but there is room for either meaning here, whereas in 2 Kings 19:35, when the Lord smites 185,000 Assyrians, we are told the results are all "dead corpses."

Exodus 21:12, 21:20, and 22:1 all make the clear distinction "whoever smites *and* he dies." Numbers 35 is careful to say it the same way. Exodus 21:18–19 states what to do if an aggressor "smites" but the victim lives. Exodus 21:26 prescribes the punishment if a slave owner "smites" the eye of their slave. But Exodus 21:15 decrees the death penalty if any child "smites" their father or mother—just for hitting them? Apparently so—the Law makes it clear when "smite" means "kill." But in Leviticus 24:17, the Law uses the unusual phrase "whoever *smites a life/soul*," a phrase also used three times in Numbers 35. To "smite a life/soul" apparently means to kill, since 24:18 speaks of paying "a life for a life" if someone smites the life of an animal. So in Leviticus 24:21, "smite" clearly means "kill."

If there is any question whether the Hebrew Bible means kill, smite, or wound, go to a concordance and dig. One final passage where the difference comes through is the very first time "smite" is used, in Genesis 4:15. In the previous verse, Cain fears that anyone who finds him shall slay him (*harag*). But in 4:15, God puts a mark on Cain, lest anyone should "smite" (*hikkah*) him in any way, killing or otherwise.

Another verb that is sometimes but not always fatal is the verb *ḥalal*, which literally means "pierced," and is virtually always rendered in Greek as *traumatizō*. Unlike *hikkah*, there are very few examples of this verb where the victim has not died. The Suffering Servant in Isaiah 53:5 was "*wounded* for our transgressions." Our Bibles read in 1 Samuel 17:52 that Philistines fell "wounded" while being chased after the fall of Goliath; why the translators choose "wounded" and not "dead" is not clear. The same is true in Judges 9:40; why "wounded" and not "dead"? Examples where *ḥalal* probably means "wounded" include Lamentations 2:12 ("as they faint like the *wounded* in the streets"), Ezekiel 26:15 ("when the *wounded* cry"), Ezekiel 30:24 ("the groaning of a wounded man"), Psalm 69:26 ("the pain of the *wounded*"), and Psalm 109:22 ("my heart is *wounded* within me").

The Hebrew words *harag* (generic "kill") and *hēmīth* (causative form of "die") are absolutely clear; they mean "kill" every time. If your concordance tells you that your verse uses one of these, you will know what it means. Also, there is *ratzaḥ*, the verb in the commandment "Thou shalt not kill," which is always fatal, and conveys the sense of "murder." The only catch is that in Numbers 35, the whole chapter serves to explain the difference between accidental *ratzaḥ* and first-degree murder. Unlike *harag* and *hēmīth*, *ratzaḥ* is never done to animals, only to humans.

All this brings new meaning to a classic passage like Isaiah 53:4, where we saw the messianic Suffering Servant as "smitten by God." Are we to focus on his suffering, or his death? With a verb like "smite," both could be in view.

24

Laughing, Playing, and Beyond Child's Play

FORMS OF THE SAME Hebrew word, *tzaḥaq*, can mean laughing, playing, or even fondling, and often, all we have is context to tell us which meaning is meant.

Tzaḥaq is used only thirteen times in the Hebrew Bible. For the purpose of this study, I will also include the verb *śaḥaq*, which is used thirty-six times, and appears to be a later spelling variation of *tzaḥaq*. (The Koehler-Baumgartner lexicon confirms this move.) For me, the key piece of evidence is Judges 16:25, where the Philistines call on Samson to "make sport" for them, a verse where both spellings of the word are used with the same meaning.

Let's begin with *tzaḥaq*. The first five times it occurs in the Bible, it is used to describe what Abraham (Genesis 17:17) and Sarah (Genesis 18:12–15) do when they are told they will conceive a child together in their extreme old age: they "laugh." The child they produce is named by the same verb: *Yitzḥaq* = Isaac, "he laughs." (The modern Israeli name Yitzḥak is simply the biblical name Isaac.)

The scene shifts temporarily in the next chapter to Sodom (Genesis 19:14), where Lot has received an evacuation order from his heavenly guests. When Lot tries to explain the order to the men who are engaged to marry his daughters, it says he seemed to them to be "joking," another shade of the meaning of *tzaḥaq*: not laughing, not playing, but "making fun" of them, as it were.

After laughter from sheer disbelief, laughter continues for Abraham and Sarah as a form of joy mixed with disbelief in Genesis 21:6 as Isaac is born. Sarah declares that God has given her *tzeḥoq* ("laughter," a noun form), and that all who hear the incredible news will "laugh" along with them.

But then the story takes a disturbing turn. In 21:9, Sarah sees her maid's son Ishmael engaged in some kind of action, and it's the same verb: *tzaḥaq*. Is he "laughing" (i.e., "mocking," as the King James renders it)? Or could it be, as the Greek reads, that he is "playing *with her son Isaac*" (notice the addition of words in the Greek)? Or is he "molesting" Isaac? That third suggestion may sound wild, but our next few verses where this word is used may give some weight to this possibility. The fact that Sarah immediately compels Abraham to cast mother and son out into the desert becomes somewhat more understandable if this was the kind of play that can put someone in jail for a long time when it is done today.

The next time we find this verb is in Genesis 26:8, where Isaac tells King Abimelech that Rebecca is his sister, but then the king later looks out his window and sees Isaac "playing" with Rebecca his wife. Our English translations have rendered this in all sorts of different ways: "sporting" (KJV), "caressing" (NAS, NIV-UK), "showing endearment" (NKJV, NIV-US), or "fondling" (RSV, NRSV). Whatever kind of "play" it was, what he saw led the king to immediately conclude that only a married couple would be doing that, not brother and sister! Keep this meaning in mind as we consider how to read Genesis 21:9 above, and as we consider the next two passages.

The next two times we find this verb are in Genesis 39, where Potiphar's wife charges Joseph with attempting to compel her into sexual misconduct. In verse 14, she states to her household that her husband has brought in this Hebrew slave in order to "make fun of" or "mock" us (the household). In verse 17, she says to her husband himself that Joseph came in "to mock/make fun of me." Considering the seriousness of the charge, "molest" would not be too strong a word for what she accuses Joseph of trying to do. Whether this nuance is what she actually intended is for you and me, the readers, to figure out for ourselves.

Other than where Samson is called on to "entertain" the Philistine crowd (i.e., make them laugh) in Judges 16:25, the final use of this spelling of the word in question is in Exodus 32:6, where, when the Israelites hold a feast for the Golden Calf at Mount Sinai, it says that they sat down to eat and drink, and rose up to "play." Again, what kind of "play" is this?

LAUGHING, PLAYING, AND BEYOND CHILD'S PLAY

Probably not bingo! It would appear to be very "adult" play, seeing that in verse 25, Moses sees that the people "had thrown off all restraint" (different verb here), "to their shame among their enemies." The Latin version says they had "stripped off their clothes" (*quod esset nudatus*). This kind of play would have made the Canaanites and Egyptians blush. "Revelry" is how the NIV and NRSV choose to translate here.

See how laughing, making people laugh, playing, and more than just child's play are all encompassed by this same Hebrew verb! Knowing this, I encourage you to read the above passages in light of these possibilities to see what fits best in your understanding of them.

The uses of the alternate spelling *śaḥaq* are often employed to speak of performing and dancing. Particularly famous are the verses where David "danced" before the Lord (2 Samuel 6:5, 21) and where the women sang "as they *were making merry*" that "Saul has slain his thousands" (1 Samuel 18:7). In 1 Chronicles 15:29, the writer uses different words for David's dancing and his unspecified "merry-making." In 2 Samuel 2:14, two teams of soldiers "perform" with swords, ending in slaughter.

Seven of the nine times *śaḥaq* is used in Job, it means to "laugh." Psalm 2:4 says, "The One who sits in heaven *laughs*." God also laughs in Psalm 37:13 and 59:9, while in Proverbs 8:30–31, Wisdom "rejoices" before God and in God's Planet Earth. The classic April Fool's Bible verse is Proverbs 26:18–19: "Like a maniac who throws firebrands, arrows, and death, is the person who deceives their neighbor and says, I am only *joking*."

There is a lot of merry-making, laughter, and mockery in the other places where this spelling of the verb is used, but no other examples that could be construed as molestation. The noun form *śeḥoq* usually means laughter (Psalm 126:2), but can also mean "laughingstock" (Jeremiah 20:7), or pleasure (Proverbs 10:23, where the wicked and the wise have two different ideas about what is "fun").

Ecclesiastes 3:4 decrees that there is a time to "laugh." Whoever said that God was a stuffed shirt?

25

Who Are You Calling Boy?

THE HEBREW WORD *NAʿAR* is commonly translated "boy" or "lad." But how old is a "boy"? How old is a *naʿar*? Let's take a look at a representative sample of the 240 times this word is used in the Hebrew Bible.

Joseph is still said to be a *naʿar* when he is seventeen years old (Genesis 37:2). Ishmael is called a *naʿar* when he is over thirteen, when he and his mother are sent away by Abraham (Genesis 21:12–20), while in the next chapter, Isaac is still a *naʿar* when Abraham is asked to offer him in sacrifice (Genesis 22:12). David is told in 1 Samuel 17:33 that he cannot fight Goliath, because he is only a *naʿar*. At Sodom, all the men of the city bang on Lot's door, both old man and *naʿar* (Genesis 19:4), a verbal pair covering the two ends of the age spectrum. Shechem, the guy who raped Jacob's daughter Dinah, is called a *naʿar* in Genesis 34:19.

But in Exodus 2:6, Moses is called a *naʿar* while he is an infant crying in his basket in the Nile. Gideon's firstborn son is afraid to slay the captured enemy leaders, because he is only a *naʿar* (Judges 8:20). Before Samson's birth, the angel says the *naʿar* shall be a Nazirite to God from the womb (Judges 13:5). In 1 Samuel 1:22, Samuel the *naʿar* has not even been weaned yet. In 1 Samuel 4:21, the newborn baby Ichabod is called a *naʿar*, as is the short-lived newborn child of David and Bathsheba in 2 Samuel 12:16. In 1 Kings 3:7, Solomon complains that he is just a *naʿar*, and doesn't know how to be a king. In 2 Kings 2:23, it is specified that some "small" *neaʿrīm* mock Elisha for being bald.

First Kings 11:28 states that Jeroboam is both "a mighty man of valor" and a *naʿar*. In Job 1:19, Job's partying children, who are adults with houses of their own, are called *neʿarīm*. The clueless young man who gets seduced by the "cougar" in Proverbs 7:7 is said to be a *naʿar*. Isaiah 3:4: "I will make *neʿarīm* their princes, and sucklings shall rule over them." When God first calls Jeremiah to be a prophet, Jeremiah answers, "Lord God, I do not know how to speak, for I am only a *naʿar*" (Jeremiah 1:6). Zechariah 11:6, the last time the word is used in the Hebrew Bible, is the only verse where the word refers to young animals rather than humans.

In Genesis 14, the word seems to mean "servants." Here it is used for Abram's trained men who fought to recover the people kidnapped from Sodom, but elsewhere the word is often used for servants of unspecified age such as Gideon's servant Purah (Judges 7:10) and Saul's servant (1 Samuel 9:5). The spies in Joshua 6:23 are *neʿarīm*, as are the fighters in the sword contest in 2 Samuel 2:14, and the executioners in 2 Samuel 4:12.

Somewhere in the late teen years, *naʿar* overlaps another word, *baḥur*, which literally means "picked/chosen man," a guy who is in the prime of his life and fit for military service. (See Isaiah 40:30, "*Young men* shall fall down exhausted.") *Baḥurīm* are always comparatively young in age, but are never children.

Naʿar has a feminine form, *naʿarah*, "girl," which is used eighty times in the Hebrew Bible. Much of the time, the word is spelled with the exact same consonants as *naʿar*; only an unwritten vowel on the end tells us the difference. *Naʿarah* is often paired with synonyms such as *betulah* (virgin) and *ʿalmah* (young, inexperienced girl—see chapter 14). Unlike *naʿar*, almost all of the uses of *naʿarah* refer to girls who are at least teenagers, including girls who are eligible for marriage. The related word *neʿurīm* is found in the famous line Psalm 103:5, "so that your *youth* is renewed like the eagle's," and Psalm 127:4, "Like arrows in the hand of a warrior are the sons of one's *youth*" (both NRSV).

The overarching characteristic of all of the uses of *naʿar* is comparative young age. For boys, that could mean anywhere from birth to late twenties. So in a verse like Proverbs 22:6, "Train up a boy [literally] in the way he should go," or Proverbs 22:15, "Folly is bound up in the heart of a boy; the rod of discipline will remove it far from him," there is honestly no way to tell exactly what age is intended, or at what age the advice no longer applies. That leaves it to you, the Bible reader, to use your God-given judgment as you seek to apply verses like these. You may even wish to add that unwritten *–ah* vowel on the end, if it helps you determine whether the verse applies equally to both genders.

As for 2 Kings 2:23, while I have heard the claim that the *neʿarīm* on whom Elisha pronounced a curse for ridiculing his bald head were actually teenage hoodlums, don't believe it. The word "small" (*qatan*) rules that out. Targeting God's prophet turned out to be as hideous a mistake for these kids as playing on the freeway.

Do not mistake this term, however, with another word for children, *banīm*, for which the masculine singular is *ben* and the feminine singular is *bat*. This is the generic word "son/daughter," which gives us no clue on age, except that the offspring must be younger than the parent. The same is true for the term *yeladīm*, which is also translated "children" and comes from the verb for childbirth.

"Youth" turns out to be a relative term in the Hebrew Bible, a word even more flexible in Hebrew than it is in English. It extends all the way from fetus to grown warrior. But the English word "child" in our Bible may be translating a word that points to parentage rather than age.

26

Does God Do Bad? Depends on What We Mean

Does God do "bad"? It depends on what we mean by "bad." The Bible teaches that God does not do what we would call moral evil. But yet at the same time, the Bible does teach that God makes stuff happen that we would call "bad" in a broad sense. When talking about a subject like this, language is everything.

The Bible has several specific words for moral evil. They include the Hebrew words *reshaʿ* (wickedness), *peshaʿ* (transgression), *ʿawon*, *ʿawen* (iniquity), and *ḥaṭaʾ* (sin), along with the Greek word *poneros* (evil). However, Hebrew also has a broad word *raʿ* that means "bad," roughly parallel to the Greek word *kakos*. *Raʿ* can mean "bad behavior" or "evil." But *raʿ* can also mean bad events or times that have nothing to do with the morality of any behavior. Let's take a look at some revealing examples of how this common but multifaceted Hebrew word for "bad" can be used.

The meaning "evil" fits the majority of the 310 uses of the noun *raʿ*, starting with its debut in Genesis 2:9 with the tree of the knowledge of good and "bad." "Knowing good and bad" was the temptation made by the serpent that led to the moral fall of humankind (Genesis 3:5). God sees that the thinking of the human heart in Noah's day was "only evil continually" (Genesis 6:5), and even after the flood, God declares that the inclination of the human heart is "evil" from their youth (Genesis 8:21).

Job is described as a man who "feared God and turned away from *evil*" (Job 1:1, 1:8, 2:3). Seven times we are told that Israel relapsed and "did evil" in the book of Judges. Twenty-seven kings are said to have done "evil" in the sight of the Lord. David confesses that he has done "evil" in Psalm 51:4. And in Genesis 13:13, we are told that the men of Sodom were "*wicked*," which is then further explained as "major-league sinners against YHWH."

But sometimes the word for "bad" does not refer to moral evil. It can refer to "bad" news (Exodus 33:4). "Badness of appearance" means "ugly" in the case of the cows in Pharaoh's dream in Genesis 41:3. "Bad" refers to yucky figs in Jeremiah 24:2, and to "bad" sores in Job 2:7. There is "bad" water at Jericho in 2 Kings 2:19, and in 2 Kings 4:41, Elisha throws flour into a poisoned pot of stew, and there was no longer "bad" (harm) in the pot.

Bad can even mean "sad" in verses like Nehemiah 2:2, where the Persian king asks Nehemiah, "Why is your face *bad*?" The Greek translation reads "evil," but the Latin renders it "sad." Ecclesiastes 1:13 says, "It is an *unhappy* business God has given to humans to be busy with." Ecclesiastes 7:3 says, "By *sadness* of face the heart is made glad." Ecclesiastes 8:9 says, "One rules over another, to the other's *hurt*." Proverbs 25:20 speaks of "one who sings songs to a *heavy* heart." And in Genesis 40:7, Joseph asks his fellow prisoners, "Why are your faces bad (= sad)?"

A number of the uses of the word "bad" are expressions of opinion. In Genesis 24:50, Laban cannot say whether the marriage deal for his sister Rebecca is "bad or good." In Genesis 28:8, we have the first example where "bad in the eyes of" means "not pleasing;" here we have the verb form "to be bad," which is used 105 times in the Hebrew Bible. When God had mercy on Nineveh, it was "displeasing" to Jonah (Jonah 4:1). Likewise, "it was bad" to Abraham when Sarah tells him to cast out Hagar (Genesis 21:11). "It was bad" to Samuel when the people demanded a king (1 Samuel 8:6). And Joshua says to the people, "If *it seems evil* to you to serve YHWH, choose you this day whom you will serve" (Joshua 24:15). All of these examples seem to involve expressions of opinion on what is pleasing or not, rather than strict moral verdicts.

But which is which is not always clear. It is surprising that 2 Samuel 11:27 simply says that David's adultery and cover-up murder "was bad in the eyes of YHWH" rather than using stronger, unambiguous language. What Onan did in Genesis 38:9–10 was also "bad" in the eyes of YHWH, but the moral issue seems to be why he did it, to deprive his brother of offspring, which was apparently "bad" enough for God to permanently strike him down.

DOES GOD DO BAD? DEPENDS ON WHAT WE MEAN

Habakkuk 1:13 declares that God's eyes are "too pure to behold evil (*raʿ*)," and Zephaniah 3:5 says that the Lord "does no wrong (*ʿawelah*)." But God does bring bad occurrences that are not morally evil and that are not inconsistent with God's character. God declares in Isaiah 45:7, "I make *shalom* (well-being), and I create *raʿ* (harm)." Job asks his wife, "Shall we receive good from the Lord, and not receive bad?" (Job 2:10). Elijah prays, "O Lord my God, have you brought bad upon this widow?" (1 Kings 17:20). In Ruth 1:21, Naomi laments that the Almighty has "brought bad" upon her. In Numbers 11:11, faced with a rebellion, Moses asks God, "Why have you done bad to your servant?" And Joshua warns Israel that if they renege on their covenant, God will "do you harm" (Joshua 24:20).

Think about the implications of all these translation options to a familiar verse like Psalm 23:4—"I will fear no bad." We can take these words as confidence not merely in the face of attack by evil, but by any form of bad.

The broad range of meaning for this generic Hebrew word "bad" (*raʿ*) should lead us to exercise caution when we run into the word "evil" in our Bibles. If you have Strong's or Young's concordance, check and see whether the generic word is being used, or a specific word for what we would call moral evil. God does not do moral evil, but God can unleash "bad," which may be consequences for sin, but may be simply part of the brokenness of the created world cursed by human sin.

And God gives us a vision in Revelation 21:1–5 of a future world where "bad" shall exist no more, in any of its forms.

27

Divine Necessity

ONE HUNDRED AND ONE times the New Testament uses a little three-letter Greek word (*dei*) that means "It was/is necessary." In the plan of God, certain events absolutely had to happen. That includes what happened on July 31, 1977, when my wife and I met and spent our first day together at Silver Falls State Park, Oregon. She was from Oregon; I was from St. Louis. God was determined to make this happen.

The risen Jesus asks the men on the Emmaus Road, "Was it not necessary that the Messiah should suffer these things, and then enter into his glory?" (Luke 24:26). Later Jesus appears to his followers and says, "Thus it is written, that it is necessary for everything written of me in the Law of Moses and the prophets and the Psalms to be fulfilled" (Luke 24:44). It was necessary. God says the cross and resurrection absolutely had to happen.

We find this term "it was/is necessary" all over the writings of Luke, both in his Gospel and in the book of Acts. When Jesus is twelve years old in the Temple, Jesus says, "It is necessary that I be in the things of my Father" (Luke 2:49). In the Parable of the Prodigal Son, the father says to the oldest son, "It was necessary that we should make merry and be glad" (about the return of your brother). (Luke 15:32) Twice, Jesus warns his followers, "It is necessary that the Son of Man suffer many things" (Luke 9:22, 17:25). Jesus says to Zacchaeus, "It is necessary that I stay at your house today" (Luke 19:5). God's got it planned, and nothing's going to stop it.

In the Upper Room, Peter tells the church "it was necessary" that Judas should do what he did, as God's word had foretold (Acts 1:16). He tells the crowds, "There is no other name (than Jesus) by which it is necessary that we be saved" (Acts 4:12). When God tells Ananias to baptize Saul, God says, "I will show him how much it is necessary that he suffer for my sake" (Acts 9:16). After Paul survives being stoned with rocks, he tells his friends, "It is necessary for us to enter the kingdom of God through many sufferings" (Acts 14:22).

As Paul looks ahead in his ministry, he declares that "it is necessary that I also see Rome" (Acts 19:21). When times get tough, and it is doubtful whether that will happen, twice an angel appears to Paul and assures him that "it is necessary" for him to stand before Caesar in Rome (Acts 23:11, 27:24), although during a storm, he predicts it will also be "necessary" for his boat to be shipwrecked on some island (Acts 27:26).

John also talks about divine necessity. John says in 4:4 that at one point, "it was necessary" for Jesus to pass through Samaria. There were plenty of other ways he could have gone (most Jews took the bypass around it), but Jesus had to go through Samaria. Jesus had to talk to the woman at the well. It was a divine necessity. Jesus tells Nicodemus that "it is necessary" for one to be born again (John 3:7) and for him to be lifted up on a cross (John 3:14). In John 3:30, John the Baptist says "it is necessary" for Jesus to increase, but "I must decrease." And in 20:9, John says they did not know the scripture, that "it was necessary" that Jesus rise from the dead.

In 1 Corinthians 11:19, Paul says, "It is necessary for there to be divisions among you, in order that those who are genuine among you may be recognized." In 1 Corinthians 15:53, Paul states that "it is necessary that our perishable nature put on the imperishable, and our mortal nature put on immortality." In 2 Corinthians 5:10, he states that "it is necessary for all of us to appear before the judgment seat of Christ." Likewise, the book of Revelation talks about future events that are "necessary", events that must soon come to pass (Revelation 1:1, 4:1).

One tiny three-letter word: "It was/is necessary." Each of these are appointments with destiny—events that absolutely had to happen according to the plan of God. Presbyterians like me believe that God is pulling the strings. We may not jump to the conclusion that God's got every last detail programmed. There are many parts of life where any number of possible scenarios could take place. But we can also say that there are certain benchmarks along the way where God's plan is destined to have its way.

It was necessary for Jesus to pass through Samaria, to speak to the woman at the well. It was necessary for him to be betrayed. It was necessary for him to be nailed to a cross. It was necessary for him to rise from the dead. These were not chance occurrences or meaningless accidents of fate. Peter says they happened "according to the deliberate plan and foreknowledge of God" (Acts 2:23).

Life is full of cases of divine necessity, cases where it had to happen that way, places where God's absolute will takes over, places where we can say that God had it planned all along. We won't always recognize those moments at the time they happen, but someday, we'll be able to look at it all in perspective and say, "It was necessary."

The Greek terms for "destine" and "predestine" (*orizō* and *pro-orizō*) convey more than signaling intention. They refer to determining or locking-in what will happen. In the Greek translation of Numbers 30, *orizō* is used for being "bound" by a vow. The Bible refers to Jesus' crucifixion as such a "locked-in" event: Jesus was "delivered by the *deliberate* counsel and foreknowledge of God" (*orizō*—Acts 2:23). "The Son of Man goes, as it was *determined*" (*orizō*—Luke 22:22). Peter preaches that Jesus' enemies joined together "to do whatsoever your hand and your counsel *predetermined* to be done" (*pro-orizō*—Acts 4:28). Peter says Jesus is the one "*ordained* of God as judge over the living and the dead" (*orizō*—Acts 10:42).

Ephesians 1:5 says that God has "*predestined* (*pro-orizō*) us unto adoption as children." The "us" to whom Paul refers is the Ephesian Christians, not the whole human race. Paul goes on in verse 11 to state that in Christ "we have obtained an inheritance, being *predestined* (*pro-orizō*) according to the purpose of the One who works all things after the counsel of his will." Paul writes to the Romans, "For whom he (God) did foreknow, did he also *predestine* (*pro-orizō*) to be conformed to the image of his Son" (Romans 8:29).

God is a sovereign God, a God who is in complete, indisputable control. We may think we have the ultimate veto power in our actions, but Proverbs 16:9 tells us otherwise: "The human heart plans its way, but the Lord directs his/her steps." We'll talk about that in our next chapter.

28

Drag Versus Draw: How Does God Bring People to Faith?

"Drag" versus "draw"—which way would be the best word to translate what Jesus says when he says in John 6:44, "No one can come to me unless the Father who sent me draws him"? And what are the implications for what we believe about God and how God operates? Does God sweet-talk us or persuade us into faith? Or does God drag us into belief, kicking and screaming, against our will?

The word Jesus uses in John 6:44 is the word *helkō*, which can mean either "draw/attract" (like a magnet) or "drag." The word is used eight times in the New Testament. The best example where the word arguably means "draw" rather than "drag" is John 12:32, where Jesus says that when he is crucified, "I will draw all people to myself."

Otherwise, the New Testament meanings of this word all lean toward "drag." In John 18:10, the word is used to describe Peter pulling his sword out of its sheath. In John 21:6, the disciples are barely able to "drag" in the net because of the huge catch of fish (see also 21:11). In Acts 16:19, the owners of the fortune-telling slave girl "dragged" Paul and Silas into court. In Acts 21:30, the mob "dragged" Paul out of the Temple, intending to lynch him. And in James 2:6, James argues that it is the rich who "drag" his readers into court. None of these examples can be easily taken to mean persuasion or attraction rather than pulling by force; indeed, the dragging is done against people's will, wherever people are involved.

The word *helkō* is used thirty-four times in the Septuagint, with similar results to be found (it is used six times there for "drawing" the sword), although the Septuagint gives us more examples that could be taken in a non-drag sense. For example, in Nehemiah 9:30, Nehemiah says that God "coaxed" them and warned them by his Spirit through the prophets. Fourth Maccabees 14:13 speaks of parental love for one's children that "*draws* everything toward sympathy from the inmost parts." Fourth Maccabees 15:11 speaks of such parental love "*drawing* the mother to suffer along with her children."

Psalm 10:9 (= 9:30 in Greek) speaks of the villain who lies in secret and catches the poor "when he *draws* them into his net." Both Psalm 119:131 and Jeremiah 14:6 speaks of "drawing" one's breath. Third Maccabees 5:49 speaks of babies at the breast "drawing" their last bit of milk. In Song of Solomon 1:4, the girl says to her beloved, "Draw me away after you!" Wisdom 19:4 says that the fate that the ungodly deserved "drew" them to a nasty end. Finally, in Jeremiah 31:3 we read, "I have loved you with an everlasting love; I have *drawn* you unto mercy."

Such is the evidence from biblical Greek. One may read the examples identified above as either "draw" or "drag." Out of the forty-two times that the word in question is used, twenty-two of them are unquestionably "drag," ten do not lend themselves to either meaning, and only ten have any chance of being taken to mean "draw." So Jesus' words can best be translated, "No one can come to me unless the Father who sent me *drags* him."

Much as we like to think of God sweet-talking us or gently attracting us into faith, the truth is that God has to drag us there. We have an approach/avoidance problem with God. We are like the man possessed by the legion of demons, who comes running to Jesus, but who screams for Jesus to leave him alone. Part of him yearns to be set free from bondage, but part of him is terrified. Indeed, even the bystanders in this account are terrified with this Jesus—instead of asking him to stay and set them free, they ask him to leave their neighborhood. Yes, elsewhere the crowds followed Jesus, and the tax collectors and sinners were drawn mysteriously to him, but at the cross, all abandoned him but a handful of women who had nothing more to lose.

We are like Lot, who cannot bear to leave Sodom, despite the fact that he knows it is about to be destroyed. The angel grabs him by the arm and drags him out of town—and don't miss the words, "The Lord was being merciful to him." When God overpowers our free will and drags us into faith, like Saul when he was struck down on the Damascus Road, God does so in mercy.

As a believer in the Reformed tradition, the doctrine of irresistible grace (which is what we're talking about) is positive and reassuring to me. God drags us into faith, and *we* can't throw it away. We in the Reformed brand of faith are totally pessimistic about our ability to choose God or do the right thing, unless God drags us into doing so. I have no faith in my own human ability. Ask anyone who's been through a Twelve-Step program, and they'll tell you: freedom from bondage comes only when we surrender to a Power higher than ourselves. Human ability will never choose God on its own.

The Reformed tradition has its own nagging, unresolved questions. What part does free will play? Are we just robots? How can we be held responsible, if God is pulling virtually all of the strings? What about those who fall away from faith? Whether one sides with the Reformed approach or with free will, both models require us to stretch one or more of the puzzle parts to make the rest of them fit. To me, the Reformed tradition gives me the most comfort. I just don't have that much faith in my own goodness or capacity to choose God. I'm glad that God made the inexplicable choice to drag me into faith.

29

What Was Wrong with Leah's Eyes?

IN THE BEAUTY CONTEST between Leah and Rachel in Genesis 29:17, we are told that Leah's eyes were "weak" (*rakkoth*), and (or "but") Rachel was "beautiful of form and beautiful of appearance." So what does that mean? English Bibles lean toward the opinion that Leah's eyes were "weak," but "soft," "tender," and "delicate" are also strong contenders for how to translate this line. Let's take a look at all the uses of this adjective in the Hebrew Bible, and you can decide for yourself. (Please note that even the translation "but" versus "and" here is entirely based on our hunch as to whether a negative comparison is being made, or simply "here is Leah, and here is Rachel," with no value judgment on either description.)

In Genesis 18:7, Abraham grabs a calf from the herd, "*rak* and good," usually translated "tender." In Proverbs 4:3, Solomon describes his earliest memories of his father's teaching when he was *rak* (tender) and the only child of his mother. Ezekiel 17:22 speaks of plucking off a "tender" branch from the top of a tree.

"Tender and delicate" is an expression to describe both men and women who then become heartless cannibals of their own children (Deuteronomy 28:54, 56). It is also used in Isaiah 47:1 in a declaration to the virgin Babylon: "You shall no longer be called tender and delicate."

The expression "tender of heart" is used in Deuteronomy 20:8, where military officers command the troops that anyone who is "fearful or tender of heart" to go home. It is also used three times in Chronicles to describe Solomon as "a boy and tender of heart" and therefore too inexperienced to run a Temple construction project, and Rehoboam (in a verbatim expression) as unable to stand up to bad advice from worthless scoundrels around him (see 1 Chronicles 22:5, 29:1; 2 Chronicles 13:7).

"Soft" is a good translation in famous lines such as Proverbs 15:1, "A soft answer turns away wrath," and Proverbs 25:15, "A soft tongue can break a bone." This meaning also fits in Job 41:3 about Leviathan: "Will he speak soft words to you?"

"Weak" seems to be the best way to translate this word in Genesis 33:13, where Jacob says he cannot keep up with the pace of his brother Esau, because his children are "weak/frail" and his flocks are nursing. A very revealing statement that uses this word is in 2 Samuel 3:39, where David makes excuses as to why he cannot punish Joab for murdering Abner, the opposing general who came to make peace: "Today I am *weak*, though I am anointed king. These men, the sons of Zeruiah, are too harsh for me." (Sounds like David owed too much to the warriors who helped put him in power!)

The related stative verb form "to be tender" is used eight times in the Hebrew Bible. In 2 Kings 22:19 (= 2 Chronicles 34:27), Huldah the prophetess says that King Josiah's heart "was penitent" (literally "was soft" as opposed to hard or stubborn). In Psalm 55:21, David says that his enemy's words "were softer" than oil, but they were drawn swords. Isaiah (1:6) says that Zion's wounds have not been "softened" with oil. And in three places, we find exhortations that the listeners' hearts should not "be soft" or faint (Deuteronomy 20:3, Isaiah 7:4, Jeremiah 51:46), plus a declaration in Job 23:16 that God had made his heart that way.

That's all the times this adjective *rak* and its related verb are used in the Hebrew Bible. So, which is it in the case of Leah's eyes: weak, soft, tender, or delicate? You make the call. Just know what the options are. The truth of God's word does not hang in the balance on which meaning we prefer.

So how does it all play out? One of my parishioners suggested that while Jacob chooses Rachel as the winner of this beauty contest at the beginning of the story, in the end Leah ends up being more loved than Rachel, perhaps because of all of the children she bore to him. I'm not so sure I agree with him, but yes, I have always thought it was curious that Leah gets buried with Jacob in the family burial cave at Qiryat-Arba, while Rachel gets buried on the side of the road on the way to Bethlehem. How crazy that the line of Jacob's royal descendants all seems to hang on a beauty contest between two sets of eyes!

If the account of Rachel and Leah is fiction, the above question is unanswerable and irrelevant (Rachel's Tomb itself would become a fictionally motivated name). But the fiction approach is unnecessary. Only the historical Jacob knows whether he ever came to truly love Leah as strongly as he loved Rachel. Their story becomes a living illustration of the downside of polygamy as a departure from God's explicit intention for sex and marriage (see my Patheos post "God's Sex Mandate: The Two Shall Become One Flesh"), as well as a living illustration of why the later Law of Moses forbids marriage between a man and two sisters simultaneously (Leviticus 18:18).

It is uncanny how God is able to use messed-up sexual behavior that is contrary to his intention, in order to achieve important long-range sovereign plans. God overturns the results of the beauty contest between two sets of eyes. God actually uses the trickery of a pushy Syrian sheep rancher to con Jacob into a marriage he never would have chosen, in order for his unwanted wife to become the mother of the future royal line, and ultimately of the Messiah.

Leah's "soft" eyes are eventually mirrored in the eyes of the earthly Jesus. But today, his eyes are a flame of fire as he awaits the appointed time for his return to Planet Earth.

30

Thief or Terrorist: What Kind of Criminal Was Crucified with Jesus?

"Thief" is too mild a word in the verse where we are told that Jesus was crucified between two "thieves" (Matthew 27:38). The same is true in John 18:40, where we are told, "Now Barabbas was a robber" (KJV). The language is too mild. Not even "bandit" has enough kick to translate the word *lēstēs*. Barabbas and his buddies who were crucified with Jesus would be better described as revolutionaries, guerillas, pirates (the landlubber variety), or (to use a modern term) "terrorists."

The difference becomes clear when we look at the alternative Greek terms. *Kleptēs* is the term for a burglar, someone who steals by being sneaky (Matthew 6:19–20). Jesus compares his coming to being like a *kleptēs* in the night (Matthew 24:43, Revelation 3:3, 16:15). Likewise, the New Testament compares the day of the Lord to such a thief (1 Thessalonians 5:2–4, 2 Peter 3:10).

Paul's sin list in 1 Corinthians 6:10 includes not only *kleptai*, but also *harpages*. A *harpax* is a literally a "snatcher," a mugger, someone who steals openly by force. The verb form is "to snatch," the same verb Paul uses for the Rapture in 1 Thessalonians 4:17 (*harpagēsometha*, "we shall be snatched up").

Our daughter describes the three Greek terms for thief as "sneaky, grabby, and stabby." "Sneaky" is the *kleptēs*. "Grabby" is the *harpax*. Now, it's time for the "stabby."

We might call the *lēstēs* a *harpax* on steroids. Today's ISIS fighters would be an excellent example, who combine robbery, pillaging, and murder with political revolution. Josephus uses *lēstēs* and its related adjectives and substantives 143 times. He pairs the *lēstai* together with the *stasiōdes* (insurrectionists, as in for example *Jewish War* 5:53). He explicitly describes as *lēstai* the Sicarii, men who circulated in the AD 50s with short hidden daggers which they used to assassinate anyone who was not part of the anti-Roman resistance (literal "cloak-and-dagger!"). Josephus also speaks of the rebels who tyrannized Jerusalem through the horrors of AD 68–70 as *lēstai*. He uses the term *lēstrikos polemos* for "guerilla warfare" (*Jewish War* 2:65).

In the parable of the Good Samaritan in Luke 10:30, the traveler to Jericho is attacked by *lēstai*. The attackers not only strip him (the robbery component), but also beat him and leave him half-dead. There is no political revolution component (of course, Jesus probably intends the story as fiction), but here it is the gratuitous violence that marks the attackers as *lēstai* and not simply *harpages* or "snatchers."

Two *lēstai* were crucified with Jesus. Barabbas (John 18:40) would have been the third, if he had not been freed by the Good Friday mob. Barabbas was being held for insurrection and murder (Luke 23:19), not stealing. We must note that neither Jewish nor Roman law prescribed the death penalty for mere theft. These men next to Jesus at Calvary were not being crucified for stealing, but for being violent revolutionaries.

The cross was a death so hideous, that both Gnosticism and Islam tried to wiggle out of the scandal thereof by claiming that God engineered a substitute for the real Jesus. For Gnosticism, they needed a substitute for the physical pain. For Islam, they needed a substitute for God's prophet to avoid the ultimate injustice.

Nice try, but it flies in the face of honest history. Who was there on the ground who was in a position to take Jesus' place, or to make it happen? Simon of Cyrene could be commandeered to carry the cross, but none of those who were carrying out the crucifixion would have allowed a substitute for the victim.

The scandal was unavoidable. It was part of the total price Jesus paid for the sins of an entire planet. The physical and emotional pain was bad enough. Cicero calls it *crudelissimi taeterrimique* (the "most cruel and terror-inspiring" penalty), while Origen calls it *turpissima* ("most obscene"). But the real pain was the penalty of hell placed on him for every one of us that was squeezed into those few hours of earthly time.

WHAT KIND OF CRIMINAL WAS CRUCIFIED WITH JESUS?

How degrading, for Jesus to suffer Rome's most hideous punishment with such dangerous, violent men! Here we have a vivid picture of the depths to which Jesus humbled himself (Philippians 2:8), from whence God highly exalted him, and gave him the name at which every knee shall bow. Let us ponder the humiliation Jesus suffered by being crucified between two terrorists, as we commemorate Good Friday and celebrate Resurrection Sunday.

31

Holiness: Being Different from a Dysfunctional World

Lent is a good time to reexamine the meaning of holiness. What exactly does it mean to be holy? The answer might surprise you.

When we say the word "holy," we often think of some kind of sinless perfection, to be a religious super-hero like Mother Teresa or someone who has reached the Hall of Fame we call "sainthood." We think of someone who scrupulously obeys a long list of do's and don'ts. We bristle when someone thinks they are "holier than thou": they don't want to hang around us, and we don't want to hang around them either. Who wants to be holy, if that's what the word means?

The word "holy" in both Hebrew (*qadosh*) and Greek (*hagios*) doesn't come with any of that baggage. It means simply "to be set apart" for a special purpose or for someone's exclusive possession. In fact, in the Hebrew Bible, "holy woman (or man)" can even mean "prostitute," one who is sacred to or dedicated to a Canaanite deity (see Deuteronomy 23:17, Hosea 4:14, 1 Kings 14:24)! In Hebrew, "holy" means the opposite of "common."

Focusing on the New Testament, the word for "holy" is used 233 times, ninety-three times in reference to the "Holy Spirit." There are holy angels, a holy city and holy place, and sixty-two times that the New Testament refers to "saints," that is, people who belong exclusively to Christ. One verse that stands out is Romans 12:1, where Paul exhorts his readers to present their bodies to God as living sacrifices, "holy" and acceptable to God.

HOLINESS: BEING DIFFERENT FROM A DYSFUNCTIONAL WORLD

The related noun "holiness" (*hagiasmos*) is used ten times in the New Testament. Hebrews 12:14 says that "no one will see the Lord" without "holiness" (or "sanctification"). And Paul gives one example of this for new believers: "This is the will of God, your *sanctification*, that you abstain from sexual immorality . . . For God has not called us to uncleanness, but in *holiness*" (1 Thessalonians 4:3–7).

The word "holy" gives the idea of being separated from the rest of the pack, to be different. Being different can be either good or bad, depending on how we look at it, and depending on the norm in question ("different from what?"). Being deviant or criminal (depending on the standard being used) is a bad way of being different from the crowd. But if you think of the world as a crooked place where you can't trust anybody and people are selfish, malicious jerks, then being different is not a bad thing at all; in fact, being different in this way can be attractive to a world that's looking for a healthier way to live.

Dostoyevsky's novel *The Idiot* is about a character who wasn't selfish or hateful or envious or spiteful or greedy or lying or sexually immoral, a guy who was so different that he gave some people the creeps. For some of us, however, such a character would be a refreshing alternative to the rest of the world around us. Where can you find such a person?

God calls us to be different. The apostle Peter quotes the Law of Moses, where God declares, "You shall be holy, for I am holy" (NRSV). God is different, and God wants us to be like God in this regard. That's why Peter urges his readers to be holy, to be different from the surrounding culture (1 Peter 1:14–16). Later in this same letter, Peter urges his readers to stop doing what the Gentiles like to do (1 Peter 4:3). Peter mentions lawless sexuality and getting bombed with alcohol, but in other parts of his letter he also mentions hatefulness, envy, lying, and hypocrisy, which are also not healthy for the soul. God wants followers of Jesus to be different from a messed-up world.

The world is looking for people who are different. They're looking for people who are selfless, not selfish; who are selfless, not because they are powerless to do otherwise, but because they don't have egos that are craving to be satisfied. Where can we find people who give or help without any wish or expectation for reward or appreciation, and who keep on giving when others quit? If you give to help a poor person and get treated ungratefully, then you'll find out whether you were really expecting a reward. Selflessness is part of what it means to be holy, to be different.

The world is looking for people who don't worship money or material goods. They're looking for people who put people before profits. They're looking for people who will take the job that pays less but will do more good. They're looking for people who aren't always measuring everything by "What's in it for me?" Proverbs 28:21 says, "For a piece of bread, a person will do wrong." The world is looking for people who won't sell out their morals or their ethics with the excuse, "I can't afford to do the right thing." That would be really different.

The world is looking for people who truly listen, who truly care. The world is looking for people who are not hateful or malicious or always angry or resentful, people who don't need to play petty games to build themselves up by tearing others down. They are looking for people whose lives are not falling apart, people who are emotionally healthy. And when they find such people, they'll want to know, "Where can I get what you have?"

Now, none of us is perfect. We all have our rough edges. We are all recovering sinners. We all still have ways where our woundedness shows itself in how we talk about or treat others. But being different needs to become the goal of our spiritual life. That's the mark of maturity. That's what we can call holiness.

Believe it or not, the world is looking for people who live the Bible's sexual ethic: sex exclusively between a husband and a wife. The world is looking for the modern equivalent of the whooping crane: couples who wait until marriage, and then enjoy each other as long as they both shall live. The world wants to see evidence that it can be done, and that the results are happier that way. It's like the Oregon joke, "Why did the chicken cross the road? To prove to the possum that it *can* be done!"

Now, there is no need to criticize those who fail or make mistakes in the area of sexuality. They've got enough pain; I don't need to add to it. That's my point. God wants us to avoid heartache. God wants the very best for our love life. That's one way where being holy, being different, pays huge emotional rewards.

More than ever before, the world is looking for people who can be trusted. They want people who don't blow off promises or commitments, people who do what they say they will do. They want people who won't pretend to be friends and then stab them in the back. As much as the world rewards posers and pretenders by falling for their sweet-talk, the world wants people who are genuine, people who will say what they mean and mean what they say, people who won't bend, fold, or mutilate the truth, even if it is costly for them to avoid doing so. People who refuse to lie are a huge part of what it means to be holy, to be different.

The world is also looking for people who believe what they claim to believe. Back in the 1700s, the famous skeptic David Hume was seen running to hear George Whitefield, the Billy Graham of that day. Someone asked Hume, "Why do you want to hear him? You don't believe what he believes." And Hume replied, "Of course I don't. But *he* does!"

The world doesn't want people who believe just because others want them to, or because it's the easy thing to do. The world is looking for people who don't back down, who don't pursue faith as a nice fairy tale that is never to be taken seriously, people who passionately believe, and who live like they believe it. That's part of what it means to be different, to be holy.

A church whose people have their act together could be powerfully attractive to a world that is looking for a better life. There are a lot of people who don't go to church because they don't see any reason to. They don't see how our lives are any different than theirs. How much change has Christ made in our lives? Has Christ given us peace and joy? Has he given us reason to live that we didn't have before? Has he made us less jerky people: less selfish, less hateful, more caring, more loving, more sacrificial, more emotionally healthy and mature? Has Christ replaced our confusion with confidence on the issues that truly matter in life? Has he broken the chains on us that enslave so many people's lives?

Show me a place where God is changing people's lives, and you'll see people breaking down the door to get into that church. You'll see communities that refuse to zone those churches out of business, because the community can't do without them. People are looking for a church that is different, and what they're looking for (I would say) is a church that is holy, whether they would call it that or not.

Here I have hopefully cast for you a new vision of what it means to be holy. It means being set apart, being different in a positive sense. In a messed up world that is sick of its own dysfunctionality (whether they realize it or not), people who are different offer a better way to live. They offer tremendous benefits to those who live around them. If you think about it the right way, being holy—being set apart—being different from a dysfunctional world—is the most attractive, appealing way to live.

32

Does God Repent? And How Should We?

THE FIRST WORD WE hear out of John the Baptist's mouth is "Repent," a word that pretty much summarizes his message. It's the same word we hear from Jesus as his first word after he returns from the desert and begins his message.

"Repent!" It's a hard word to ignore. Yet it is also a word packed with meaning far beyond what we may have imagined.

The Bible's term for repentance (*metanoia*) is a much broader term than simply turning from sin. The verb "repent" (*metanoeō*, used thirty-four times in the New Testament), and its companion noun (used twenty-two times in the New Testament), both mean literally a "change of mind," a 180-degree turn that includes turning away from evil, *and* turning away from previous thinking, either good or bad.

The word "repent" in its noun and verb forms is found chiefly in Matthew, Luke, Acts, and Revelation (zero times in James or John!). The word "repent" is found in landmark passages such as Acts 2:38, where Peter commands the crowd at Pentecost, "Repent, and be baptized!" Paul says in Romans 2:4 that God's kindness is meant to lead us to repentance, to turn away from our self-destructive path and to turn toward God. And in 2 Peter 3:9, we are told that God desires that no one should perish, but that all should reach repentance. In Revelation, five whole churches are called to repent.

The New Testament meaning of repentance contains monumental changes of both mind and of behavior. Jews who heard the Gospel needed to change their minds about how to reach God: no longer by law, but by faith. They also needed to change their minds about Jesus, which was a huge change for those who believed that God could never become one of us. Greeks and Romans needed to throw away their idols and worship one true God, plus they needed to make major changes in their lifestyles. For us today, salvation also involves repentance. It requires a change of mind. We come to love God more than we did before. We come to hate sin more than we did before.

Repentance means that life will be a lifelong process of getting our act together and rooting out what is not from God. It requires us to think again: "How could I have done that differently? How could I have avoided losing my temper, or surrendering to desires that are not good for me? Are there thoughts or words or actions I need to turn away from, to repent of?"

But some people define repentance to mean getting rid of every single sin in our life. They make that a requirement for salvation, and if we turn from sin and then sin again, they'd say we have not truly repented. If that's true, we are all lost. 1 John 1:8 says, "If we say that we have no sin, we deceive ourselves, and the truth is not in us" (NRSV). Repentance is the willingness or determination to forsake sin, a refusal to declare a ceasefire against sin. But if a person is happy with sin and wants to continue in sin, unrepentant sin can be a major sign that a person has never truly been saved. It's not whether we sin, but whether we want to stay in sin. Sin is like weeds; we'll never finish rooting them out of our lawn, but we're crazy to want to plant more of them!

However, repentance is a need that goes beyond getting rid of sinful behavior. It also includes changing our mind on beliefs and behaviors that are not sin, they are simply mistaken. Mistaken beliefs or mindsets don't work. They don't get us where God wants us to go. They're like a bad map. Who wants to go through life guided by a constantly mistaken road map?

Repentance: a change of mind, a change of heart, a 180-degree U-turn that includes turning away from evil, *and* turning away from wrongheaded thinking that no longer works for us (if it ever did). God's call to repent calls us not only to turn from sin, but to rethink all we thought we knew to make sure it comes from God and not us, and to unlearn what we need to unlearn, so that we can be free to do what God calls us to do in the here and now.

Now, what about God? Can or does God repent? Does God ever need to do so? Does God change, or does God remain forever the same? A related question: Can God change his mind or his plan? Can God change his rules, or is everything that God decrees an expression of unchanging divine principle? My problem with a God who can change is that we end up with a God who is always changing his mind about matters that ought to remain settled. God may issue a firm statement this year, but who knows what God will think next year? Who can rely on the word of such a God?

Bedrock principles do not change with time. Don't tell me racism is wrong today but was OK with God in the days of Jim Crow, or that sex outside of marriage was wrong in the Victorian age but is right today. If racism is wrong today, it was always wrong, whether we acknowledged it or not. Don't drag God into it, as if God can't make decisions for all time on such matters.

Objection: Doesn't God set aside the Law of Moses for Christians? And what about God's seeming turnabout on eunuchs, who are forbidden to enter God's sanctuary in Deuteronomy 23:1, but who receive a blessing from God for doing what is right in Isaiah 56:4-5?

Jesus is central to our answer to the question of God's law. Jesus has harsh words for anyone who would relax even one tiny letter of God's law (Matthew 5:17-19, Luke 16:17), yet according to Mark (7:19), he was implicitly "cleansing all foods" (i.e., setting aside the kosher food laws) when he declared that nothing that goes into a person can defile a person (Mark 7:14-23). In another radical move, Jesus says that God permitted divorce in the Law of Moses "because of your hardness of heart . . . but from the beginning it was not so" (Matthew 19:8).

How can Jesus make such breathtaking pronouncements? The answer is because Jesus is our authorized interpreter of God's law. Being God in the flesh, he is uniquely qualified. This means that no one else is authorized to issue any such radical updates to God's law. And because Jesus says that he came not to abolish the Law, but to fulfill it (Matthew 5:17), Jesus makes all of the Hebrew sacrifices unnecessary, because he has already offered the ultimate sacrifice that takes away sin on the cross (Hebrews 9:23-26).

Isaiah's declaration of God's blessing on eunuchs who keep the Sabbath and do what pleases God does not throw out the ceremonial law on who is permitted to enter the Temple, any more than Jesus' heart for the handicapped (Luke 14:13-14) sets aside the ceremonial laws about them (Leviticus 21:16-24). Isaiah 56 and Luke 14 merely clarify that God still loves these classes of people, and that the Temple ceremonial laws are not intended to convey otherwise.

Can God change his mind (= repent)? We are told that God "was sorry" (*niham*) to have made the human race in Genesis 6:6, that God "was sorry" to have made Saul king (1 Samuel 15:11), and that God "changed his mind" about destroying Israel (Exodus 32:14) and Nineveh (Jonah 3:10—all the same word). But the Bible also says that God is not a human being, that he should repent (same word—see Numbers 23:19, 1 Samuel 15:29).

The same word can and does cover both meanings. Should we suppose that God did not know what would happen under Plan A, so God changes his mind to a better plan? I prefer to think that God's mind does not change, but that God enacts first one course of action that God knows will be disastrous, then switches to a better course of action, purely by sovereign choice, to prove what would happen under Plan A, while grieving that Plan A had to be done at all.

Does this solution sound complicated? To me, it sounds a lot better than the prospect that God keeps making bad decisions that have to be changed. How do you make a deal with a God who can't be counted on to keep promises? If those promises were conditional, we can understand why they would be withdrawn, but not if they were mistaken planning on God's part.

Having a God who can always change his mind and issue a new revelation may be convenient, but it's not true to life. Having a God who is too much like us always leads to messy complications. How much better to have a God who does not change! (Malachi 3:6).

33

Life on the Straight and Level

To call anything or anyone "crooked," we first have to know what a straight line is. The Hebrew Bible has a word for it, used in some very famous verses: "There is a way that seems *right* to a person" (NRSV). "Everyone did what was *right* in their own eyes." "In all your ways acknowledge him, and he will *make straight* your paths" (NRSV).

The Hebrew concept of being "upright," doing what is "right," the opposite of crookedness, is expressed by the word *yashar*. From this word, we get the name of a lost book quoted twice in the Hebrew Bible, the Book of Jashar (Joshua 10:13, 2 Samuel 1:18), the "Book of the Upright," which is evidently used as one of the multiple sources for the Hebrew historical books.

Permeating the uses of *yashar* (both verb and adjective), and the related noun *mēsharīm*, are the ideas of "straight" and "level." We can clearly see this in the way the Greek translates this word as *eutheis* or "straight" in Psalm 7:9. *Mēsharīm* (used nineteen times in the Hebrew Bible) is a synonym of *tzedeqah* (righteousness) and *mishpaṭ* (justice). In the Psalms, "equity" is a good way to express the levelness intended here: God is the one who judges the peoples with *mēsharīm* (Psalm 9:8, 58:1, 75:3, 96:10, 98:9, 99:4). If anyone wants to find equality in the Bible, they should look for it here. Also, in Proverbs 23:31 and Song of Solomon 7:9, *mēsharīm* is used adverbially to describe wine that goes down "smoothly."

Also related to *yashar* is the noun *mīshor*, which means a flat land, a plain or plateau. In 1 Kings 20:23, the Arameans believe that Israel's God is a god of the hills, but can be defeated if they fight him on the *mīshor*. Here the meaning of straightness or levelness in this root is most clear.

The intensive and causative verb forms of the *y-sh-r* root often mean "to make straight", as in Psalm 5:8, "Make thy way straight"; Proverbs 3:6, "[God] will make straight your paths"; and Isaiah 40:3, "Make straight in the desert a highway for our God" (NRSV). In 1 Samuel 6:12, the oxen "go straight" to Israelite territory carrying the ark of God. And in numerous passages (Judges 14:3, 14:7; 1 Samuel 18:20, 18:26; 2 Samuel 17:4; 1 Kings 9:12; 2 Chronicles 30:4), this verb means to "be pleasing", i.e., straight or "right" in one's eyes.

Which brings us to our third meaning, conveyed by the adjective form (119 times) that is often used as a noun. *Yashar* is a synonym of *tzaddīq* (righteous), and goes with *tob* (good) and *tam* (blameless—Job 1:1, 1:8, 2:3). Possibly the most common use of *yashar* is to denote what is "right" or "upright." A classic verse where it is used this way is Judges 21:25, where Israel without a king was such a mess that everyone did what was "right" in their own eyes. Another classic verse is Proverbs 14:12 (= 16:25), where there is a way that seems "right" to a person, but its end is the way to death. Ecclesiastes 7:29 says that God originally made humans "upright." Twelve times in Kings and ten times in Chronicles, we are told that a king did what was "right" (versus "evil"). Those who are "upright" are spoken of twenty-five times in Psalms and twenty-five times in Proverbs, not counting the expression "upright of heart" (seven times in Psalms).

Less common, but perfectly logical, meanings for *yashar* include 2 Chronicles 29:34, where the Levites were more "conscientious" (upright) than the priests in purifying themselves for the Passover. In 2 Kings 10:3, Jehu tells the capital city of Samaria to choose someone "qualified" (the "right" person) to reign in place of their dead king.

Our final two examples echo more of the straight/levelness contained in the meaning of *yashar*. In Jeremiah 31:9, we are told of a "straight/level" path/way in which people will not stumble. And in Micah 3:9, the prophet speaks of those who pervert/make crooked all *yasharah*: straightness, levelness, equity, or simply "what is right."

There are many words for what is good, righteous, or just in the Hebrew Bible. The *yashar* root carries with it a clear sense of what is straight and level, to a world with plenty of crookedness to go around, a world where everyone does what is "right/straight/level" in their own eyes.

Look out for the God who is holding the plumb line! God may have a different idea of what is "right" than we may kid ourselves into thinking.

34

What's the Difference between Spirit and Soul?

Pentecost is the perfect time to explore the use of the word "spirit" in the New Testament. Our journey will prove to be more complicated than we may have imagined, but at least we can sort out where the meaning of the word is clear, and where the word's meaning is too debatable to insist that we always know exactly which sense is intended.

The Greek word *pneuma* comes from the verb *pneō*, "to blow," from which we get the triple meaning "wind/breath/spirit," the meanings that Jesus plays on in John 3:8: "The *pneuma* blows where it wills, and you hear the sound of it, but do not know where it comes from or where it goes. So it is with everyone who is born of the *pneuma*."

Is it the "breath" or "spirit" of life from God that is meant in Revelation 11:11 and 13:15? Here we see that the word can be notoriously imprecise, because sometimes it simply refers to elements of the non-material sphere, but sometimes it refers to the non-material element in a human personality or an animal, and sometimes it refers to specific personal beings. When the risen Jesus appears in Luke 24:37–39, "spirit" means "ghost" of a dead person (see also 1 Peter 3:19).

In 2 Thessalonians 2:8, we are told that Jesus will destroy the Lawless One with the "breath" of his mouth. But when he dies on the cross, we are told that he gave up his *pneuma* (Matthew 27:50, John 19:30), which could mean either that his life functions quit, or that the non-material part of him departed. The "spirit" is what one surrenders when one dies

WHAT'S THE DIFFERENCE BETWEEN SPIRIT AND SOUL?

(Luke 23:46, Acts 7:59), and the return of which constitutes resurrection (Luke 8:55). In John 11:33, the "spirit" is the seat of one's emotions: Jesus is "deeply disturbed in the spirit." (We find a similar use in Mark 2:8 and 8:12, John 13:21, and 2 Corinthians 2:13.)

While a *psychē* always belongs to a body, or once did so, spirits are often disembodied, and must enter a body from outside thereof. Both angels and demons may be described as "spirits." 1 John 4:1 says "Test the spirits, whether they are from God." Paul writes in 2 Thessalonians 2:2 that believers should not be misled by a "spirit" which claims that the day of the Lord has already come. Paul also complains in 2 Corinthians 11:4 that his readers are too willing to receive a different "spirit" from the one they received earlier. That's why one of the spiritual gifts in 1 Corinthians 12:10 is the ability to distinguish between spirits.

By contrast with *pneuma*, the Hebrew Bible term *ruah* is only used twice in the plural to refer to personal beings; the other seven plural uses are references to the "four winds." *Ruah* is seen in Ezekiel 37:9 to have the same triple potential meaning as *pneuma*. We have a similar puzzle in both languages in Genesis 1:2: was it the "Spirit," "wind," or "breath" of God that was hovering over the waters of creation?

"Spirit" also has a figurative meaning. "Blessed are the poor in [the realm of] spirit" (Matthew 5:3). Galatians 6:1 speaks of correcting a fallen believer "in a spirit of gentleness" (same expression in 1 Corinthians 4:20). The same figurative meaning is found in Revelation 19:10, "The testimony of Jesus is the spirit of prophecy" (NRSV). Several times in Revelation (1:10, 4:2, 17:3, 21:10), John says he was literally "in spirit"—the lack of the Greek article "the" may or may not point us to the meaning "in the spirit world" rather than under strong influence of the divine Spirit. Similarly, Paul tells the Colossians that although he is absent in body, he is with them "in spirit" (Colossians 2:5—see also 1 Corinthians 5:3–5).

Sometimes soul and spirit are used as synonyms (Luke 1:46–47), but sometimes they clearly speak of different components of a human being. "May your spirit and soul and body be kept sound and blameless" (1 Thessalonians 5:23 NRSV)—how do we distinguish the first two? What is the "dividing point between soul and spirit" in Hebrews 4:12? Hebrews may be referring to "spirit" as the presence of the Holy Spirit inside a believer, but if Paul means the Holy Spirit in his prayer for the Thessalonians, why or how does the Spirit within them need to be kept "sound and blameless"? Perhaps he means not to grieve or drive the Spirit out of their lives (Ephesians 4:30).

When New Testament writers intend to contrast the two dimensions, they always contrast "spirit" and body rather than "soul" and body. James 2:26 states that "the body without the spirit is dead." In 1 Corinthians 7:34, the unmarried woman worries about "how to be holy in body and spirit," while in 2 Corinthians 7:1, Paul urges his readers to put away "every defilement of body and spirit." Jesus says to his slumbering followers in Gethsemane, "The spirit is willing, but the flesh is weak" (Matthew 26:41).

God is Spirit (John 4:24). What that means: God does not have a material body. Latter-day Saint authorities would disagree. In the official Latter-day Saint scriptures, *Doctrine and Covenants* 130:22 states that "The Father has a body of flesh and bones as tangible as man's." This belief is central to the whole of Latter-day Saint theology. Our belief that God is Spirit and not flesh (which makes the Incarnation of Jesus so astounding) makes a huge difference. The fact that God is Spirit is one of the foundational attributes of God.

The Hebrew scriptures speak of the "Spirit of God." Moses yearns that God would put his Spirit upon all of God's people (Numbers 11:29). God then promises through the prophet Joel to pour out his Spirit upon all flesh (Joel 2:28). But the New Testament names this "spirit" as the Holy Spirit, in a way probably not intended in the few such occurrences of this expression in the Hebrew Bible (Psalm 51:11). The pouring out of this Spirit on all believers, not just a privileged few, is the fulfillment of Joel's prophecy that we celebrate at Pentecost.

Ultimately, the New Testament brings us to understand that God's Spirit is not merely an aspect of God like the voice or mind of God, but is also worthy of worship, not as another deity, but as one of three persons who together are one God (Matthew 28:19, 2 Corinthians 13:13). The Holy Spirit is the One through whom God and Jesus dwell within every believer. The Holy Spirit is the One who empowers us to live a holy life (Romans 8:1–13), and who leads us into all truth (John 16:13). No one ever set out to invent this triune understanding of God, but the whole of God's word, inspired by God's Spirit, compelled us to this conclusion.

35

Soul or Life? The Double Meaning of *Psychē*

SOUL, OR LIFE? SUCH is the choice we must make in translating the New Testament word *psychē*, which we have borrowed into English as our term "psyche," and from which we get our word "psychology."

Psychē is easily distinguished from the other two Greek words most often used to mean "life." *Zōē* (from which we get "zoology") is best described as the antithesis of death. It is the only word used for eternal life (John 3:16), the word to which Jesus turns in John 6:35 when he says "I am the bread of life." *Bios*, a word used only ten times in the New Testament, is used for physical existence, including livelihood; the poor widow in Mark 12:44 gave her whole *bios* to God (two copper coins), while the hemorrhaging woman in Luke 8:43 spent her whole *bios* on doctors (not all Greek manuscripts have this comment). Jesus says that the seed that fell among thorns gets choked by the pleasures of one's *bios* (Luke 8:14).

"Conscious personal experience" would be a good nine-syllable way to describe *psychē*. Because it can be read either "soul" or "life," we should try to keep that double meaning in mind wherever possible. In a verse like Matthew 2:20, "those who seek the child's life are dead," we know Herod was just trying to kill Jesus, not condemn his "soul" eternally. Likewise, when Jesus says, "Don't worry about your life" (Matthew 6:25 = Luke 12:22), his next few words make it clear that he is talking about our earthly existence; plus, we can hardly imagine Jesus telling us not to be concerned about the eternal destiny of our soul! Both Acts 15:26 and Philippians 2:30

refer to people who have risked their "lives," not their eternal states. And in Revelation 12:11 ("they did not love their lives unto death"), again, the emphasis is on one's share in earthly experience.

In Matthew 10:28, Jesus warns us about those who can kill the body and can't kill the *psychē*, a verse which seems to indicate that a "life" cannot be extinguished as easily as a flame can be. In Revelation 6:9, John says he saw the souls of those who died (we never see a dead "spirit" in the Bible). So in verses like these, the *psychē* refers to the inner person that lives on after death, as we see in Peter's quote from Psalms in Acts 2:27 (NRSV), "You will not abandon my soul to Hades," where the context is what God will do for the psalm writer after death.

Numerous verses employ *psychē* to refer to the inner person and its condition. Hebrews 6:19 speaks of the "anchor of the soul," while James 1:21 speaks of the "word that is able to save your souls," and 1 Peter 1:9 speaks of "the salvation of your souls." First Peter 2:11 speaks of forces "which war against the soul." The writer of Hebrews 12:3 is concerned for his readers, "lest you become weary in your souls." In the same sense, Jesus says in Matthew 26:38 (= Mark 14:34), "My soul is sorrowful, even to death," while he says in John 12:27, "Now my soul is troubled," (NRSV) and in Matthew 11:29, "you shall find rest for your souls" (NRSV). Acts 4:32 stretches our imagination by telling us that the earliest believers were "one soul" (= one mind), which is also Paul's prayer for his readers in Philippians 1:27.

In Matthew 16:25–26 (= Mark 8:35–37 = Luke 9:24), Jesus uses the word *psychē* ambiguously four times: "Whoever wants to save their life will lose it, but whoever loses their life for my sake will find it. For what shall it profit a person to gain the whole world and lose their soul/life? Or what shall a person give in exchange for their life/soul?" A similar use may be found in James 5:20, where restoring a sinner from error "will save his soul/life from death." In all of these verses, one can argue for either meaning.

When Jesus says in Matthew 20:28 (= Mark 10:45), "The Son of Man came . . . to give his life as a ransom for many," both meanings of *psychē* come into play, in that Jesus not only suffers physical death but also bears the penalty of hell in his soul in his atoning work on the cross.

In a verse like Luke 12:20 ("Fool! This very night your soul/life is required of you!"), both meanings are possible, but the eternal destiny of the man's "soul" is easy for the modern reader to see as the issue.

In John 15:13, "Greater love has no one than this, that a person lay down their life for their friends," Jesus is probably not recommending that we should offer ourselves to be eternally condemned. The same is true for John 10:11 NRSV ("The good shepherd lays down his life for the sheep") and 1 John 3:16 ("we ought to lay down our lives for our brothers/sisters").

Sometimes the word "soul/life" is used simply as a means of counting individuals, where our Bibles may gloss over the presence of the word. So Acts 2:41 reports that on the first Pentecost there were added to the church "about three thousand souls," and in Acts 27:37, it says "we were 276 souls in the ship." In the same sense, Paul writes in Romans 13:1, "Let every soul be subject to the governing authorities." In Acts 2:43, "fear came upon every soul," this sense is less clear. In Revelation 16:3, the expression extends even to animals: "every living soul (= creature) in the sea died."

In Colossians 3:23 (= Ephesians 6:6), Paul tells slaves, "Whatever you do, work from the soul" (i.e., from the heart of who you are), much like in the Greatest Commandment, "Love the Lord . . . with all your soul" (Matthew 22:37 = Mark 12:30 = Luke 10:27). The same intensity would seem to apply to the meaning of 1 Thessalonians 2:8, where Paul reminds his readers, "We were pleased to share with you . . . our own lives."

First Thessalonians 5:23 is the only New Testament verse where "spirit and soul and body" are all differentiated. In 1 Corinthians 15:45, Paul writes, "The first Adam became a living soul; the last Adam became a life-giving spirit" (*pneuma*). Finally, in Mary's Magnificat (Luke 1:46–47 NRSV), "My soul magnifies the Lord, and my spirit (*pneuma*) rejoices in God my Savior," we have a poetic pair, where the two terms *psychē* and *pneuma* are not identical (see previous chapter).

36

Koinōnia: What We Share in Common

WHAT EXACTLY IS "FELLOWSHIP"? We tend to think it means "socializing," when we read that the earliest church spent so much of their time doing it (Acts 2:42). But then, what does the "fellowship of the Holy Spirit" mean in Paul's description of the triune God in 2 Corinthians 13:13? What does Paul mean when he says he wants to know the "fellowship" of Christ's sufferings? (Philippians 3:10). And what does Paul mean when he uses the same word to say that the bread and wine of the Lord's Supper are a "communion" in the body and blood of Christ? (1 Corinthians 10:16). Since we can't ask Paul at the moment, let's figure it out by looking at the various ways this word is used in the Bible.

Koinōnia is one of the best known New Testament Greek words, and one of the least understood. Back in the 1970s, "koinonia" (fellowship) groups were all the rage in churches, until they led to "koinonitis" (a humorous name for a "disease" where groups were too tight-knit to make room for others). *Koinōnia* and its related words (*koinōneō, koinos, koinoō, koinōnos,* and *koinōnikos*) are used fifty-six times in the New Testament. Meanings for these words range from "fellowship" to "partnership" and even to the adjectives "common" and "unclean."

The basic meaning of this word group that holds all of the various meanings together is "sharing" or what we "hold in common." The verb *koinōneō* means precisely that: "to share." Galatians 6:6: "Let the one who is taught the word *share* in all good things with the one who teaches." "Do not *share/participate* in the sins of others." (1 Timothy 5:22) "Rejoice insofar as you *share* Christ's sufferings" (1 Peter 4:13). Second John 1:11 says that whoever greets the false teacher or welcomes them into their home "*shares* in their wicked deeds." Paul writes that rich believers should be "rich in good deeds, generous, *willing to share*" (*koinōnikos*—1 Timothy 6:18), and should "*contribute* to the needs of the saints" (Romans 12:13). Paul tells the Philippians that "no other church *partnered/shared* with me in giving and receiving" (Philippians 4:15).

"Sharing" of their total lives is a good way to translate the *koinōnia* to which the earliest church devoted themselves in Acts 2:42. Such a deep and meaningful relationship also seems to be in view in 1 John 1:3–7, where believers who "walk in the light" and not in darkness have true "fellowship" with the Father and the Son, and with one another. It's the flip side of 2 Corinthians 6:14: "What *fellowship* has light with darkness?" Such a relationship is incompatible, we are told. In Galatians 2:9, the Jerusalem apostles give Paul and Barnabas the "right hand of *fellowship/partnership*" (rather than the left foot of rejection!). The way Paul speaks of the "fellowship of the Holy Spirit" is like the Stoic philosopher Epictetus wishing for "fellowship with Zeus" (*Discourses* 2.19); Paul rejoices that we actually have such a relationship with the one true God.

Paul tells us that the bread and cup we share in the Lord's Supper are a "communion/participation/sharing" in the body and blood of Christ (1 Corinthians 10:16). That's why Paul warns them in 10:20 that to knowingly eat food sacrificed to idols is to be "partners" (*koinōnoi*) with demons. When Paul says he wants to know the "fellowship" of Christ's sufferings (Philippians 3:10), he means he wants to *share* in what Jesus suffered on behalf of us all.

Koinōnia also is often used for sharing of material goods: "Do not neglect doing good and *koinōnia* (which probably means *sharing* rather than companionship), because such sacrifices are pleasing to God" (Hebrews 13:16). Paul writes that the Greek churches were pleased to make some "contribution" for the relief of the Jerusalem saints (Romans 15:26—see also 2 Corinthians 9:13: "the generosity of your *sharing/contribution*"). So when Paul says he is thankful for "your *partnership* in the Gospel" (Philippians 1:5), he may mean either companionship *or* financial sharing.

The related noun *koinōnos* means "partner," as in Luke 5:10 ("partners" with Simon) and in Matthew 23:30 ("we would not have been *partners* in [shedding] the blood of the prophets"). Hebrews 10:33 says that "you were sometimes publicly exposed to insults and persecutions, and sometimes were *partners* of those so treated." Here is also the word that is used where Peter says we can become "*partakers/sharers* of the divine nature" (2 Peter 1:4), and where Paul writes that "just as you are *partakers/sharers* of [our] suffering, so also [you may be *partakers/sharers*] of [our] comfort" (2 Corinthians 1:7).

The related adjective *koinos* means "common," as it does where we read that the earliest church had all material goods in "common" (Acts 2:44), or where Paul calls Titus a true son in a "common" faith (Titus 1:4). Surprisingly, the same word is also often used to mean "profane," "defiled," or "unclean." Paul is persuaded by the Lord Jesus that nothing is "common/unclean" in itself (Romans 14:14). The Pharisees are shocked that Jesus and his followers eat with hands "defiled" (Mark 7:2–5). In Acts 10:14 (= 10:28), Peter reminds God that he has never eaten anything "common" or unclean. Hebrews 10:29 declares how horrible it is for someone to treat Christ's blood as a "profane/common thing." Revelation 21:27 declares that nothing "common/unclean" shall enter the Holy City. Note that the Greek of the New Testament is called by the name *Koinē* or "Common" Greek, not a holy Greek.

Our takeaway from this study is that *koinōnia* or "fellowship" is a word to describe the bond between people who share one important identity that unites them across what divides them, like Cardinal baseball fans, or American citizens who meet in a foreign country; they may be at odds with each other elsewhere, and may have nothing else in common, but what they do share creates a meaningful bond between them.

The early church was composed of slave and free, dirt-poor and rich, Jews, Romans, and barbarians, women and men, who had nothing else in common but Christ, but what they did share was powerful. Part of why that was true, of course, is because they were talking about the same Jesus, and not wild or grotesque distortions. Unless we are talking about truly the same Jesus, we reduce the meaningfulness of what we share across our diversity. But when we are indeed celebrating the same Jesus, what we share in common becomes all the more amazing.

So fellowship is really all about sharing: not only our Savior and our relationship with him, but also our hearts, our joys and burdens, and even our time and material goods. Genuine fellowship should produce a mutual encouragement that sustains an otherwise isolated soul, which is why Hebrews 10:25 urges us not to forsake the habit of meeting together. The test of how genuine our fellowship may be is how much sharing we can truly do between us. Can we share our burdens? Will people listen, and will people care, as they are able? Can we be transparent as we share? Is it safe to share what's in our hearts? The quality of our fellowship, our ability to truly share, to give and receive as fellow members of Christ's body, will be what leads the outside world to declare, "God is truly among you!"

37

Be Ye Perfect? Exactly What Does Jesus Mean?

"Be perfect, therefore, as your heavenly Father is perfect." (Matthew 5:48 NRSV) Perfect? What does Jesus mean? Or are we reading Jesus wrong? If Jesus means what we mean by perfection, we are toast—which could be true. But there are other nuances to the Greek word used here in Matthew 5:48 that can give us some hope.

The adjective *teleios* is used nineteen times in the New Testament, to which we must add related nouns and verbs which we must consider. *Teleios* has three basic meanings: perfect, mature, and complete. Knowing these options can help tremendously when we encounter verses that contain one of these words in our Bible.

We find this same word in Jesus' challenge to the Rich Young Ruler in Matthew 19:21: "If you wish to be perfect, go sell what you have and give to the poor, and come follow me." In Jesus' aforementioned command to "Be perfect," Jesus has just challenged his audience to love their enemies. In both of these examples, Jesus is setting the bar sky-high for those who think they have "arrived" in their walk with God. As Jesus says, and then proceeds to unpack, in the Sermon on the Mount, "Unless your righteousness exceeds that of the scribes and Pharisees, you shall by no means enter the kingdom of heaven" (Matthew 5:20).

Hebrews 6:1 (NRSV) urges us, "Let us go on toward perfection." Is this a realistic possibility, or could "maturity" be more what the writer has in mind? Paul writes in Colossians 3:14 that love is the "bond of

BE YE PERFECT? EXACTLY WHAT DOES JESUS MEAN?

perfection." But in Philippians 3:12, Paul says that he himself has not yet been perfected. In all of these instances, "maturity" might be a better way to translate what the writer has in mind.

"Maturity" could be what Jesus is aiming at when he says "Be perfect." Hebrews 5:14 says that "solid food is for the mature." In 1 Corinthians 2:6, Paul says "We speak to those who are mature," while in 1 Corinthians 14:20, he writes, "In evil be babies, but in thinking be adults." In Ephesians 4:13, Paul speaks of the time when "we all come to mature adulthood," while in Colossians 1:28, he states that his goal is "to present every person mature/perfect in Christ." Maturity is a tricky judgment to make, of course, unless we are willing to concede that we all have a long way to grow.

The word for "perfect" can also mean "complete." A clear example is 1 Corinthians 13:10, "When the perfect comes, the partial will be abolished." This meaning is closely connected to the meaning of the related verbs (see below). "Perfect love casts out fear" (1 John 4:18 NRSV) indicates a love that has completed the process of transforming a person.

The writer of Hebrews has a lot to say about how perfection happens. Hebrews 5:9 says that Jesus was "perfected" by learning obedience through what he suffered (see previous verse, as well as 2:10 and 7:28). Hebrews 7:19 declares that the Law perfected nothing. Hebrews 9:9 teaches that sacrifices are not able to perfect the conscience, and Hebrews 10:1 adds that the Law can't do it either. But Hebrews 10:14 states that by a single offering Jesus has "perfected" us. And Hebrews 11:40 and 12:23 speak of being made "perfect" when we reach the completion of our journey in life.

James 1:4 uses this word twice in one short sentence. The first time, we are told to let patience have its "perfect work" = "full effect," while the second time the word seems to mean perfect or mature. James 3:2 says that "if anyone does not stumble in word, he is a perfect/mature/complete human" (what an understatement!). And James teaches in 2:22 that faith is "perfected" (= completed) by works. The same sense occurs in the four times it is used in 1 John, including 4:18: "Whoever fears has not been perfected in love."

The verbs related to the adjective "perfect" are *teleō*, "finish, bring to end" (used twenty-eight times in the New Testament), and *teleioō*, "finish" (used twenty-three times), all based on the noun *telos* or "end." In John 19:28, Jesus sees that all is now "finished," and so as he dies, he cries in verse 30, "It is finished!", a word that can also mean "Paid in full!" (See Matthew 17:24 and Romans 13:6 for the use of this verb to mean paying off one's tax bill.)

Numerous familiar scriptures employ this verb for perfection or completion. Paul writes in his famous last words in 2 Timothy 4:7, "I have *finished* the race." Jesus predicts in Matthew 10:23, "You will not have *finished* going through all the towns of Israel before the Son of Man comes." Paul tells us Galatians 5:16 that if we walk by the Spirit, "you will not *fulfill* the desires of the flesh." The Lord tells Paul in 2 Corinthians 12:9, "My power is *made perfect* in weakness."

Revelation 15:1 declares that after the seven bowls are poured out, "the wrath of God *is complete*." This verb is used to mark both when God's word is fulfilled (Revelation 17:17) and when Jesus has finished speaking (Matthew 7:28). The sense of God's love completing its objective can be seen in 1 John 2:5 ("Whoever keeps God's word, truly the love of God *is perfected* in him") and 4:12 ("If we love one another, God remains in us, and his love *is perfected* in us").

John Wesley is alleged to have taught that sinless perfection is not only possible, but to be expected in this life. However, in his pamphlet *A Plain Account of Christian Perfection*, Wesley writes that "'sinless perfection' is a phrase I never use," but he defines "sin properly so called" as only "a voluntary transgression of a known law," not including involuntary transgressions and/or "mistakes."[1] I remember this explanation from my Nazarene aunts years ago. I define sin much more broadly, including not only what we do, but what we fail to do, and even who we are when we are sitting still.

Clearly, perfection, maturity, or completeness can only be a relative term in this life. Completeness can only come when we have completed our journey.

---

1. Wesley, *Christian Perfection*, 17.

38

The Dark Side of the Word *Shalom*

EVERY SEMINARIAN WHO TAKES any Hebrew is proud that they have learned the word *shalom*. Now, they know the word for "peace"! Little do they realize that the word *shalom* has a dark side; it has hidden shades of meaning that are anything but peaceful.

Yes, students quickly discover that *shalom* means more than absence of military or social conflict. *Shalom* is a word that describes wholeness (Isaiah 53:5), health (Psalm 38:3), prosperity (Psalm 35:27), and well-being (Genesis 37:14). When the Shunammite woman is asked if all is OK with her, she simply says, "Shalom" ("it's OK"—2 Kings 4:26). When biblical characters (and modern Israelis) meet, they ask about each other's *shalom* (Exodus 18:7). In Esther 2:11, Mordecai stays close to the palace to stay informed about Esther's *shalom*.

Many times the adjective form *shalēm* is used to refer to a heart that is "completely" or consistently "loyal" and not divided. Examples include 1 Kings 8:61, 1 Kings 11:4 (versus 1 Kings 15:14), and 2 Chronicles 15:17 and 25:2. Hezekiah pleads that he has walked before God with a "whole/complete" heart (2 Kings 20:3 = Isaiah 38:3).

Moses commands altars to be built with stones that are "whole/complete" (*shelomoth*—Deuteronomy 27:6, Joshua 8:31). In 2 Chronicles 8:16, we are told that the work on the house of YHWH was "complete." In Genesis 15:16, God says that the iniquity of the Amorites is not yet "complete." Nehemiah 6:15 uses the verb form, "The wall *was complete*." In Job 23:14, Job says that God "will complete (*yashlīm*) what he has appointed for me."

115

The term "peace offerings" (*shelamīm*) is also rendered as "offerings of well-being/wholeness."

One landmark verse where the meaning of *shalom* embraces all of the above meanings is Jeremiah 29:7: "Seek the *shalom* (welfare) of the city where I have sent you into exile, and pray to the Lord on its behalf, for in its *shalom*, you will find your *shalom*." In the same vein, in Job 9:4, Job asks, "Who has ever resisted [God] and prospered (or "come out OK"—*wayyishlam*)?"

But social justice proponents rightly point out that *shalom* cannot coexist with evil and injustice. Such obstacles to *shalom* must be eliminated. We find this meaning in the verb form of *shalom*. Its stative form (Qal) means "to be whole/be at peace." In its transitive forms (Piel, Hifil), it means "to establish peace" (2 Samuel 10:19). And that may include: restitution (Exodus 21:34), the repayment of debts (2 Kings 4:7), and the settling of scores (Proverbs 20:22). Ouch! Here is where we see the politically incorrect side of *shalom*, the dark side to which I refer. The verb form of *shalom* is used eleven times in Job, and six of them have to do with payback.

Who would have imagined that the *shalom* root would be found in this famous line? "Vengeance is mine, and *shillēm*—recompense!" (Deuteronomy 32:35 NRSV). A few verses later, we find Deuteronomy 32:41—"I will repay (*ashallēm*) my enemies." But the repayment meaning is not always negative. In Isaiah 44:26, the verb refers to the fulfillment of God's intentions to rebuild Jerusalem. In 2 Chronicles 5:1, the verb refers to Solomon "completing" his work on the Temple. The *shalom* verb is also a common way to express fulfillment of a vow (Psalm 65:1). In fact, the name Meshullam (used seventeen times in the Hebrew Bible) is a Pual participle of the verb, a name that means "Repayment," a name that may have been given to persons who were donated to service in the Temple as payment for a vow.

"Peace" is just one of the options by which we may translate the term *shalom* when we encounter it. Sometimes, it is entirely a matter of opinion whether peace, wholeness, welfare, well-being, or all of the above are being conveyed in any instance where the word is used. And yes, some of the extended meanings of the *shalom* root are anything but peaceful. If we really want to describe "peace" as in absence of violent conflict, we would do better to go to the root *shaqaṭ*, which is used in Joshua 11:23 where the land "had rest" from war, and in 2 Kings 11:20, where the city "was quiet" after the overthrow of Athaliah. But that word might not fit in all of the wonderful scriptures where *shalom* is used.

39

Lawlessness: What Happens When Law Itself Becomes Lawless?

LAWLESSNESS IS NOT WHERE people commit crimes, but when law itself is dismantled by those who are in power. Congress or a court issues an order to a government leader, and the answer they get is, You can't make me! If Congress won't authorize the money, spend it anyway. Who's going to stop us? You don't like our immigration laws? Throw the flood gates open—who's going to stop a mob of ten million? And if you try to arrest an immigrant criminal in our city, we'll throw you in jail.

Lawlessness is uglier than sin itself. It's ugly when we get the idea that no one can stop us from evil.

Lawlessness is a concept found in explicit form only in the New Testament. There is no word for being "anti-Torah" in the Hebrew Bible. Our concept of law is a Greek concept. The word for law is *nomos*, and the antithesis to it is *anomia*, a word used fifteen times in the New Testament and 217 times in the Greek Old Testament.

Anomia is first used by Euripides in the fifth century BC. Its adjective form, *anomos*, is first used by Sophocles around the same time, and its adverb form *anomōs* is first used by Euripides. In pagan Greek, *anomia* could mean hostility to religion. Plato uses the word to refer to people who do not know the moral law. The term can be used to refer to actual deeds that are against a law, or an attitude that rejects being ruled by any kind of law outside of one's self.

In the Old Testament, five times *anomia* translates the Hebrew term *zimmah*, a word for shocking immorality such as Leviticus 19:29 (pimping your daughter) and 20:14 (sex with both a woman and her daughter). It also translates the term *shiḥēt* (to act corruptly—Deuteronomy 31:29). The vast majority of the time, it translates ʿ*awon*, the garden-variety term for "iniquity."

Perhaps the most famous use of *anomia* in the New Testament is in reference to the notorious "Lawless One" in 2 Thessalonians 2:3–4 (Paul's Antichrist by another name), "who opposes and sets himself above every so-called god or object of worship." First John 3:4 equates all sin with "lawlessness." Second Corinthians 6:14 asks, "What partnership can there be between righteousness and *anomia*?"

Jesus predicts in Matthew 24:12 that in the last days, "because lawlessness (*anomia*) is multiplied, most people's love will grow cold." While lawlessness could happen in any age, Jesus says it will dramatically increase at the end of the world as we know it.

Jesus says he will say to many souls on the Day of Judgment, "I never knew you. Depart from me, all you who practice *anomia*" (Matthew 7:23). He goes on to say in Matthew 13:41–42 that he shall gather all who practice *anomia* and cast them into the furnace of fire, where "people shall weep and gnash their teeth."

Despite the fact that John equates the two (1 John 3:4), *anomia* seems to be a step beyond *hamartia* ("sin"). The differences are degree and attitude. "Sin" seems to be used for moral failures due to weakness, but "lawlessness" seems to be used more for intentional rejection of moral restraint of any kind, a bold defiance of all moral authority.

Jesus' prediction that lawlessness would increase exponentially is coming true while we watch. It's not murder, or drugs, or our sexual free-for-all, or the plunder of property. It's the dismantling of law itself.

One element of lawlessness can be found in the writings of Saul Alinsky, hero of both Barack Obama and Hillary Clinton. Probably the most disturbing chapter of Alinsky's book *Rules For Radicals* (which I own and have read) is his eleven-point defense of his belief that the end always justifies the means. Alinsky believes that questions like conscience and morality are the luxuries of those who can afford not to suffer. He claims that all great leaders (even Lincoln!) have always invoked "moral principles" to cover "naked self-interest" dressed up as freedom, human rights, and

WHAT HAPPENS WHEN LAW ITSELF BECOMES LAWLESS?

higher moral laws. Alinsky even goes so far as to say, "Democracy is not an end; it is the best political means available."[1]

Let that claim sink in: the end always justifies the means. A lawless attitude if there ever was one! That explains a lot of recent American history.

Another element of lawlessness today is a theory known as critical legal theory. Critical legal theory argues that all law is politics. The law is just a tool to protect the wealthy, a tool of power. The law and the nation's Constitution are designed solely to keep people down. The law is just a product of political competition between winners and losers. The rule of law is merely a form of oppression. The Constitution is a mechanism for rich white guys to keep their power. So the object of the game is to strike down the current unjust law (which is unjust simply because we say so), and to replace it with another arbitrary set of rules that places another group in power (namely, us).

The metasthesizing of *anomia* into our nation's legal system is just a symptom, although (practically speaking) it is also a serious threat to justice on the society-wide level. Ultimately lawlessness is not a political issue. It is a spiritual issue.

Do we believe that there is a higher law and a Lawgiver to whom we are all accountable? (That was the reason we added "under God" to the Pledge of Allegiance, to set us apart from Communists who believed they were accountable to no one.) And are we willing to submit to human checks and balances to restrain our will to unilateral power?

God help us if we treat law (divine or human) as nothing but a tool of power, to be placed in our toolbox, right next to Mao's barrel of a gun. That's the way of the Lawless One.

---

1. Alinsky, *Rules for Radicals*, 47.

40

Oppression: Stomping on the Powerless

Oppression is when powerless people get stomped on by those who have legal, political, or economic power. God's law commands us repeatedly not to "oppress" the widow, the orphan, or the alien, the groups who were the most vulnerable to exploitation.

There are several different terms for "oppression" in the Hebrew Bible. Two of them are used in the same sentence in Exodus 22:21. One of them (*laḥatz*) means to press someone hard. It is used for Balaam's donkey shoving Balaam's foot against a stone wall. It's also used for when the Amorites shove the tribe of Dan back into the hills after they try to settle in the coastal plain. The other word (*toneh*) is a word that means to "exploit" someone. This word is used in Leviticus 25:14, where it says that in selling land, Israelites are not to "exploit" one another by charging more than the land is worth.

Another common word for oppression (*ʿashaq*) clearly means to practice extortion. Another word (*ʿinnah*) means to humble or subdue someone by treating them harshly. In Isaiah's famous line "Seek justice, correct oppression" (Isaiah 1:17), the word is a rare word that means "ruthlessness." And in Isaiah's famous line "to let the oppressed go free" (Isaiah 58:6, NRSV/NJKV), the word means literally "those who have been crushed."

One example of the use of power to coerce was (the company known at the time as) Twitter's lawsuit against a small Des Moines company who held the copyright on the use of the word "tweet." Twitter sought to simply

OPPRESSION: STOMPING ON THE POWERLESS

crush the small company's right, because it had the muscle to do so. That's how oppression works.

Eminent domain could be cited as another example of oppression. Leviticus 25:23 proclaims that all land belongs to God, and cannot be confiscated. The story of Naboth's vineyard shows that even wicked king Ahab understood that he did not have eminent domain over the inalienable rights of Naboth to his ancestral inheritance (1 Kings 20:1–6). Only Jezebel, a Canaanite who had no moral hang-ups, sees the issue through modern eyes.

Deuteronomy 23:17 commands Israel not to exploit (*toneh*) escaped slaves, who were powerless and completely at the mercy of their hosts. Leviticus 25:14 also commands Israelites not to *toneh* their neighbor when selling land by unfair pricing.

What is a fair price or wage? Other contemporary law codes such as the Law of Hammurabi and the Law of Eshnunna gave official fair prices for wages, rent, and even doctor's fees; the Hittite Law even gives a list of fair prices for merchandise. The Torah gives us none of these specific fair prices. I wish it had done so, but at least by not doing so, it avoids the problem in our U.S. Constitution of stating prices that are now woefully outdated. Even if the Torah had given us such prices, they would be useful for us only by comparison in the context of the time period in which it was decreed.

So, is a fair price always whatever the market can bear? There seems to be a difference between the price of a Super Bowl ticket or the price of lodging that night in that city, neither of which are necessities, versus the price of necessities after a hurricane. Proverbs 11:26 would appear to apply here: "The people curse those who hold back grain [in order to gouge the public], but a blessing is on the head of those who sell it" (NRSV).

The verb *laḥatz* is used to describe the way the Egyptians treated the Hebrews, involving forced labor and violence. In Leviticus 25:44–46, where the Israelites are permitted to enslave pagan nations, Moses insists that slaves who are fellow Israelites must not be treated with "harshness." Here, the word used is *parek*, the same word used for how the Israelites themselves were treated in Egypt (Exodus 1:13–14).

God's commands on how to treat aliens in Israel deserve special attention. In Deuteronomy 24:14, Israel is forbidden to practice the exploitation (*'ashaq*) of immigrants that prevailed in virtually all surrounding cultures at that time, which was similar to today's treatment of illegals by smugglers, or by employers who exploit the immigration status of their workers with threats to deport them if they complain of unjust working conditions.

Any monopoly creates the kind of power that can lead to oppression, whether it be centralized health care (where who gets a kidney or heart operation may become a matter of political favoritism), or whether it be business versus union labor, a case that can work either way, depending on which side has collected more coercive power. One critic of unions writes that nobody has a moral right to force anyone to employ them at the price they demand, or to forcibly prevent the employer from hiring others. He says, "The attempt to use violence to force an employer to pay a desired non-economic wage is clearly robbery."[1] Both employers and unions have at times been guilty of using the kind of coercion that God's law would call oppression.

It is from God's word that we derive the principle that might does not make right. Without God's word, naked power is answerable to no one.

---

1. Rushdoony, *Institutes of Biblical Law*, 508.

41

Does God Care about Justice More Than about Sex?

> "The Hebrew and Greek words for justice are used over 1000 times in the Bible. Compare that to the words for sexual sin, which are used less than 100 times . . . If we Christians obsessed over justice and mercy like we do over sexuality we just might change the world."—Lance Ford, Facebook, 2019

I CHALLENGE THAT CLAIM: both the numbers, and the method involved. Counting how many times a word is used is not a reliable way to determine what is important to the divine author of Scripture.

You'd think that what is important to God could be found in the Ten Commandments. There, sexual sin outnumbers injustice 1–0. Or look at the New Testament sin lists in Mark 7:21–23, Romans 1:26–32, 1 Corinthians 6:9–11, Galatians 5:19–21, 1 Timothy 1:8–11, and the lists of who is excluded from the Holy City in Revelation 21:8 and 22:15. In them, I find fornication, adultery, and homosexual behavior, but hardly any attention to the issue of justice.

In one of Paul's very earliest letters to a newly planted church, the first command he gives them from Jesus is, "For this is the will of God, your sanctification: that you abstain from *porneia* (sex outside of marriage—see chapters 18 and 20 of this book)." He goes on and says, "Therefore, whoever rejects this, rejects not human authority but God." (Read 1 Thessalonians 4:1–8 for the entire context.)

Porneia is condemned in eleven books of the New Testament, where forms of the word are used fifty-five times. *Krisis* (Greek for "justice") is used forty-seven times, but in the New Testament, it almost always means "judgment" (a politically incorrect part of the New Testament message).

The standard Hebrew Bible word for justice is *mishpaṭ*. It is used 425 times in Scripture. However, the word has many other meanings that make up the majority of times this word is used. In the plural, it often refers to regulations or God's "judicial decisions" (Exodus 21:1). It can mean "(legal) right" or "court case," and it often means "custom" (2 Kings 11:14). But it most often means "judgment," from which most of the other meanings come.

I find 133 times where *mishpaṭ* does mean "justice," plus another nine where it could mean either "justice" or "judgment" (like Deuteronomy 32:41 or Judges 4:5). That's not a thousand, even if we add all 157 uses of the ambiguous word *tzedeqah*. But *tzedeqah* is better translated "righteousness." Often, *mishpaṭ* and *tzedeqah* are used together in a way that indicates that they refer to two different spheres of right behavior. If *tzedeqah* ever means "justice," it is in a minority of cases. So much for the "1000+" statistic.

Yes, *mishpaṭ* is used in some powerful classic passages, such as Isaiah 1:17 ("Seek justice, correct oppression") and Micah 6:8 ("What does the Lord require of you, but to do justice . . . ?"). Justice is a major character trait of God, which undergirds our entire sense that someday, the wrongs of this evil age will be righted, a concept without which it is only too easy to lapse into the cynical despair of Malachi 2:17.

Although unfortunately God has not spelled out exactly what justice looks like in enough concrete examples to solve most of our intense modern debates about it, justice is important to God. But so is sexual morality. Jesus was tougher on that subject than the Torah. The reason is because the disregard of biblical teaching on sex does tremendous social and emotional damage. Maybe that's why God has more explicit teaching on the subject of sex in the Torah and New Testament than God gives us about what it means to do justice.

So the quote at the beginning of this chapter about the word count on justice versus sex in the Bible is nonsense, on both counts. The sad fact is that most people don't have the time or the inclination to check it out and see whether the claim is true, which it is not.

42

The Immigrant in Hebrew Law

To what extent can we apply the Bible's teachings on loving the immigrant to today's illegal aliens? How comparable is the Hebrew *gēr* ("immigrant, sojourner, resident alien") to today's immigrant?

Who exactly are the *gērīm*? The best book on this subject is Christiana van Houten's *The Alien in Israelite Law* (see bibliography). The Israelites were "aliens" in Egypt, as were the Patriarchs in Canaan. In Moses's law, the alien is a *non*-Israelite, as made clear by the roadkill law in Deuteronomy 14:21a: the Israelite must obey the kosher law, but may give the meat to an alien or sell it to a rich foreigner.

The alien is to receive the same generosity as the widow and the orphan. The triennial tithe and the first fruits are given to the alien and to others in need. God declares that leftover crops "belong" to the alien and the poor. Yet in Leviticus 25:47, a Hebrew may sell himself to an alien, which means that some of them were *not* poor.

The *gēr* was not a full citizen. There is no evidence that the *gēr* could hold land in Israel, or participate in legal matters. The *gēr* and the citizen remain rigidly distinguished. A *gēr* can become a citizen only by conversion, i.e., circumcision. The *gēr* may celebrate the Feasts of Weeks and Sukkoth, but has neither the right nor the obligation to celebrate Passover, since he/she did not come out of Egypt.

But the *gēr* was obligated to avoid offenses that would bring down God's wrath on the whole community. This includes breaking the Sabbath, consumption of blood (Leviticus 17:10), sacrifice to Molech (Leviticus 20:2), and blasphemy (Leviticus 24:16).

The alien can cry out to God (Deuteronomy 24:14–15) and expect to be heard. But because aliens cannot claim legal rights in court, they must depend on others to defend them, because they are not "insiders." That's why God issues the blanket command not to torment or pressure the alien, who is powerless, whether rich or poor (Exodus 22:21, Leviticus 19:33, Deuteronomy 23:17).

One theme that comes through loud and clear as we examine the ninety-three uses of *gēr* in the Hebrew Bible is that the *gēr* must *obey the law*. In Deuteronomy 31:12, the alien "shall learn to fear YHWH your God and observe diligently all the words of this law." In Leviticus 18:26, neither citizen nor alien shall do "any of these abominations" listed in this chapter. Several times Moses's law insists, "You shall have one law for the alien and for the citizen" (Leviticus 24:22 NRSV; see also Numbers 15:15–16; and 15:29). And in Numbers 15:30, we are told, "Whoever acts defiantly, whether native or alien, reviles YHWH, and shall be cut off from their people," meaning, they shall be expelled or deported, as I have argued in my dissertation "Cut Off From (One's) People." (To cross our modern border without legal permission can hardly be an accident, and is almost always an act of deliberate defiance.)

Much of the substance of the immigration debate hangs on the meaning of the verb in the command not to "oppress" the *gēr*. The pro-illegal-immigration crowd wants to define oppression as broadly as possible. But the language, in context, does not permit us to equate oppression with enforcement of legitimate laws. While it is true that many immigrants in ancient Israel may have been fugitives from punishment elsewhere, the only non-extradition clause found in the Torah is for runaway slaves (Deuteronomy 23:15–16), not for murderers or even for political refugees. There is no obligation in the Torah to protect any immigrant other than runaway slaves from being deported to their country of origin for crimes they have committed.

In cases where the Hebrew verb *'ashaq* is used (Deuteronomy 24:14), the NRSV correctly translates the verb as referring to "extortion." In other words, Israel is forbidden to practice the exploitation of immigrants that prevailed in virtually all surrounding cultures at that time (similar to today's treatment of illegals by smugglers, or by employers who exploit the immigration status of their workers with threats to deport them if they complain of unjust working conditions). The causative form of the verb *yanah* (Exodus 22:21, Leviticus 19:33) conveys a similar meaning: to exploit or mistreat by rip-off. This is a far cry from claiming that "oppression" means enforcing modern immigration law. To claim that illegal immigrants have an inalienable right to be here in America, based on Scripture, is a stretch far beyond what the meaning of *gēr* will allow.

The real issue is not our willingness to welcome the immigrant. Let's make it easier to immigrate legally. The one thing we have a right to expect is that immigrants obey the law. We are told these are just good, upstanding, law-abiding people who have broken only one unjust law. But if a person willfully breaks our immigration laws, they are much more likely to break our traffic laws (Why do I need a license? Why can't I drive drunk?), our tax laws (why pay them?), and our criminal laws (armed robbery, murder—try and stop me!).

Those who appeal to Joseph and Mary's refugee status forget why they ever went to Bethlehem: they were obeying an inconvenient law they could have easily blown off. And they fled to Egypt for reasons already permitted under current immigration law: to escape the murder of their child. Joseph and Mary are models of the law-abiding immigrant, not the illegal immigrant.

We should have immigration laws like Mexico's, which are far stricter than Arizona's. All immigrants to Mexico are required by law (laws which are not always enforced) to undergo background checks, and show proper papers if they are suspected of being in Mexico illegally. They are forbidden to work without permission, and will be deported if caught. The truth is that our immigration laws are already far more generous than those of other countries who criticize us.

The illegal immigrant has been compared to the person who breaks into your home, then claims that they have the right to stay, then claims that we must provide their living. Readers may judge for themselves whether the comparison fits.

One of the curses on a nation that abandons YHWH (Deuteronomy 28:43) is that "the *gēr* among you shall rise higher and higher, while you shall sink lower and lower." When illegal aliens have grown so powerful that they have created a double standard that allows them immunity from laws which the rest of us have to obey, we might want to think deeply about what is happening to us, and why.

Sadly, the issue of illegal immigration makes it harder for us to focus on ministering to those who immigrate legally. Yes, we are called to share the love and Good News of Jesus Christ with them! Jesus commanded us to go to the ends of the earth to do so; now, he has brought the ends of the earth to us! And recent conversions of large numbers of Muslims in Europe give us a glimpse of what can happen when we welcome the immigrant in our midst.

43

How to Define Hate

In Orwell's novel *1984*, Big Brother's regime has a daily ritual called the "Two Minutes' Hate," where everyone stops and fires up their rage, then returns to what they were doing.

In recent years, we have seen, not a Two Minutes' Hate, but a 24/7 hate conducted against a former U.S. President. The hate never stops. It comes from many who claim to oppose hate, but have never looked in the mirror. Many of those who accuse the former President of being full of hate have a log of hatred in their own eye.

Likewise, those like me who do not hate the former President feel considerable animosity toward those who do hate him. Alas, when I say "animosity," I fear I am playing word games, trying to weasel out of confessing my own hatred. Or am I? How do we define "hate"? To answer that, a biblical word study on the word "hate" is in order.

The verb *śanēʾ* is used 148 times in the Hebrew Bible. Most of the time, it simply means a strong dislike or opposition to a person or object (such as evil). The most instructive sound bite is Leviticus 19:17, which teaches, "You shall not hate your brother in your heart." ("Brother" here means blood relative, and since we are all blood relatives, we can extend this command to how we treat everyone.) The next verse completes the thought: "You shall not take vengeance or bear a grudge against any of your people, but you shall love your neighbor as yourself." (NRSV) This verse capsulizes what God wants us to do universally.

There are a few quirky exceptions to how this verb is used. In Genesis 29:31 and Deuteronomy 21:15, the verb is used to mean the relatively "unloved" spouse in cases where a man has more than one wife. This non-absolute meaning of the verb is helpful in making sense out of two additional otherwise thorny passages.

In Malachi 1:2–3, God says, "Jacob I loved, but Esau I have hated." If we believe the whole Bible, including "God is love," we must conclude that "hate" is being used here in a relative way. The same is true in Psalm 139:21–22, where David asks, "Do I not hate those who hate you, O YHWH? And do I not loathe those who rise up against you? I hate them with complete hatred; they have become to me my enemies."

The best I can do is to classify this as relative hatred. Leviticus 19:17 is the verse that teaches us how to do Psalm 139:21–22. Yes, we are to hate what God hates, including all kinds of evil, but we are to love people.

Relative hatred is the best way to explain Jesus' thorniest use of the verb "hate." In Luke 14:26, Jesus teaches that whoever does not "hate" their own parents, spouse, children, relatives, and even their own life "cannot be my disciple." Jesus is calling us, not to despise our loved ones or our lives, but to love *him* more, like the relative love described in "No one can serve two masters," where one cannot help but "hate the one and love the other" (Matthew 6:24).

The Greek verb *miseō* (as in "misogynist," someone who hates women) is used forty times in the New Testament. Central to Jesus' teaching is Matthew 5:43–44, where Jesus rejects the idea that the command to love our neighbor leaves us free to "hate" our enemy. Instead, Jesus gives us sky-high teaching that meets all of the historical criteria of authenticity: "Love your enemies."

According to Luke 6:27–29, loving our enemies includes doing good to those who hate us, blessing those who curse us, praying for those who mistreat us, and offering the other cheek to those who slap us, and more goods to those who rip us off. (I'm not sure if he would include providing a sword to those who would kill us.)

Love our enemies? You don't have to like someone, to desire the best for them, to care about them. Apply the 1 Corinthians 13:4–8 test. Love is not "irritated" (*paroxynetai*). Love "does not calculate/keep a record of wrong" (*logizetai*), which is admittedly hard not to do in today's political environment, where evidence for why we oppose someone is always demanded. We must cut others as much slack as we want them to cut for us.

HOW TO DEFINE HATE

Love "does not rejoice in wrong, but rejoices with the truth." (Proverbs 24:17–18 says, "Do not rejoice when your enemy falls, and do not let your heart be glad when he stumbles, or else the Lord will see it and be displeased and turn his anger away from him/her.") Are we glad when the leader we oppose gives us another piece of *skubalon* to throw at him/her? Are we disheartened, or relieved, when that person is exonerated?

Love "bears all things, always trusts (has faith), always hopes, always endures." Here we are pushing our finite human limits. But certainly hate can be measured by whether we always assume the worst or the best about the people we do not like. Hate can poison or distort what we hear, particularly what I call "Catch-22 Hate," a hate that automatically condemns the person no matter what they do.

In *Aboth de Rabbi Nathan* (one of the rabbinic writings), a rabbi puts his followers to the test. He has them watch as he begins talking to a woman, takes her into a room and shuts the door, then comes out and takes a ritual bath. Then he asked them if he had done anything evil. They said no; for each questionable element of what they saw, they had a logical innocent explanation. Then the rabbi makes his point: "Always judge everyone with the scales weighted in their favor."

The anti-police crowd (*and* their supporters) have a lot of repentance to do before they can condemn anyone else for their hate. Someone who hates white people may do an unsurpassable job pointing out what's wrong with white people, but they will do a completely ineffective job persuading them to take it to heart.

We must all draw our own conclusions about the best policies for our nation, and who would do the best job implementing them. How morally "good" or "bad" a leader happens to be may not be the bottom line by which we should measure. But by all means, let us not vote based on hate. Let us not vote for policies we know are bad, simply because we hate the person on the ballot who opposes them. Let us do our utmost not to read evil assumptions into what people say or do. Let us strive not to rejoice in the evil we hear about someone, but try to assume the best, not the worst.

44

Favoritism: God Hates It

FAVORITISM: GOD HATES IT. The Bible says that God is not a "lifter of faces" (Acts 10:34, Romans 2:11, Ephesians 6:9, Colossians 3:25, James 2:1). God doesn't check your face first to see what color or gender or economic class you are, to see if your face is pretty or ugly, or to see if you are on a preconceived friends or enemies list. Or as Dr. Martin Luther King put it, God judges not by the color of one's skin, but by the content of one's character.

The term *prosōpolēmpsia* used in the above New Testament passages was totally unknown in pre-Christian Greek. It was a word coined by the early church!

The Law of Moses says in Deuteronomy 16:19, "You shall not pervert justice. You shall not show partiality. And you shall not take a bribe, for a bribe blinds the eyes of the wise, and subverts the words of the righteous." We find the exact same definition of bribery in Exodus 23:8. The Bible is not forbidding us to pay more money to a customs agent in a foreign country to get quicker service, which may be no different than paying the postal or delivery service more money to deliver your package quicker. The evil that God forbids is whatever favors or gifts we may use to change what people see (to "blind the eyes") or to change what they say (to "subvert their words").

There are no teacher's pets with God. There is no one for whom God bend the rules, lowers the standard, or gives preferential treatment. The Jews found that out in Romans 2:11, where Paul shoots down their belief that God would cut them more slack than non-Jews; they need a Savior, just as much as the Greeks and Romans do. Likewise, slaveowners thought God would judge them more leniently than slaves, but Paul warns them both in Colossians 3:25, "for the wrongdoer will be paid back for what they have done wrong, and there is no partiality (*prosōpolēmpsia*)" toward either master or slave.

James the brother of Jesus urges believers not to show partiality (*prosōpolēmpsia*) to the rich in their meetings, while showing much less favor to the poor person in shabby clothing (James 2:1–4). It is tempting for churches to ignore or avoid people who don't fit the profile of who we want to hang out with. Perhaps we are afraid they may repel people whom we want to attract, or that they may become a bottomless pit of requests for help. Or we may think, "What can they contribute to our church?" But James's words give us little excuse not to extend such persons our fellowship and care. Indeed, when God sends us such people, God may be watching to see if God can count on us as agents of God's grace.

What a scripture for today's world! From today's crony capitalism, to "good-old-boy" (or "good-old-gal") systems in the church, to judges who fail to recuse themselves, to countless other conflicts of interest, the issue of favoritism or partiality is intensely relevant in an age like ours where who-you-know matters more than the merits of your case. Issues of bias and preferential treatment abound in the workplace, in the halls of government, in the community, and in the church.

It is scary. I see bias and favoritism in myself, and I struggle to resist it. What scares me more is the ways I may be blind to it. I also see the same evils in self-proclaimed social justice warriors who claim to crusade against those evils.

In the political world, it's amazing how the sultans of spin change their tune, depending on whether the public figure has an R or a D behind their name. Those rich, evil One Per-Centers are evil only if they are Big Oil or Wall Street, not if they have names like Amazon or Google. Is the difference a matter of the content of their character, as I am sure some will argue? Or are these actually glaring examples of checking people's faces first?

Why is the murder rate so high among urban African-Americans against each other? Is it racism to point out the obvious? No, I would argue that to excuse or ignore this evil is to do the work of the Klan for them. That is truly racist: to use the color of one's face as an excuse for evil. Why the evils of corruption, injustice, and resulting poverty are so prevalent in certain places is a scandal regardless of color. And it is a subtle form of racism to excuse those evils. It is racism to either incarcerate *or* release someone based on the color of their skin, regardless of which color is shown favor.

To what extent is "prosecutorial discretion" (choosing to prosecute some cases and not others) just a legal excuse to practice blatant favoritism? Do we have a two-tiered system of justice, where a political party determines which crimes or which riots will not be tolerated? Does the news media practice *prosōpolēmpsia* in which crimes it chooses to either cover or cover up? Do crime victims with pretty faces get more sympathy from the public than ugly ones?

Avoiding the evil of favoritism—to show favor to someone, or to call an evil what it is, without checking their face for race, gender, economic class, or political party—is notoriously difficult. Nobody said justice was easy. Instead of branding everyone we disagree with as a racist or as sexist or deplorable, we need to first root out the evil within ourselves. God is not a "lifter of faces." Neither should we be.

45

Comfort, Encourage, Exhort, or Beg?

IF THERE IS ANY New Testament word where the meaning varies wildly from sentence to sentence, and where how to translate the word becomes a matter of opinion, it is the verb *parakaleō* (used 109 times in the New Testament) and its companion nouns *paraklētos* (five times) and *paraklēsis* (twenty-nine times). It's a handy word to have in your Greek vocabulary as an average reader as you read your Bible, so that you can decide for yourself what the word means in a given passage.

The basic meaning of *parakaleō* is to "call alongside," the meaning from which all of the other meanings come: to comfort, to encourage, to exhort (give someone a pep talk), and even to beg someone to grant a request. It's a matter of degree, and as a reader of God's word, you may choose to give the word a different slant than the Bible version you happen to be using. When translating *parakaleō* and its related nouns, there may be no single "correct" way to translate them, unless if we were to ask the original author or speaker what they had in mind.

One intriguing example where *paraklēsis* ("comfort") is used is where Luke translates the name Barnabas. Luke tells us that the Aramaic nickname *Bar-Nebīyya* (literally "Son of Prophecy") means "Son of Encouragement" or "Son of Exhortation" (Acts 4:36). Already, we have a word that can mean either option. "Exhortation" fits better with the original Aramaic meaning; a prophet is one who exhorts. But the meaning "encouragement" could equally apply in the case of the Barnabas we know from the book of Acts, who comes alongside Saul to help him when the early church is afraid to trust or welcome a former killer of Christians, and who later speaks up for John Mark when Paul does not wish to take him as a missionary partner.

As early Latin-speaking Christians from Tertullian to Augustine have pointed out, the word *paraklētos* (often rendered "comforter") is even sometimes used to mean "defense attorney" (Latin *advocatus*), one who is "called alongside" to help a defendant in court. Such appears to be the meaning in 1 John 2:1, where even the King James Version reads, "If anyone does sin, we have an advocate with the Father, Jesus Christ the Righteous One." And John writes in the next verse that Christ is not only our defense attorney, but the atoning sacrifice for our sins, as well as for the sins of the entire world.

The term *Paraklētos* is best known as one of Jesus' titles for the Holy Spirit, "the Comforter," whom Jesus calls by that name in John 14:16, 14:26, 15:26, and 16:7. The Holy Spirit hence becomes the One who is called alongside of us to comfort and help us in Jesus' place.

Many times *parakaleō* and *paraklēsis* clearly mean "comfort." Paul proclaims in 2 Corinthians 1:3–4 that God is "the God of all comfort, who comforts us in all of our affliction," so that we can comfort others. Jesus says in the Sermon on the Mount, "Blessed are those who mourn, for they shall be comforted." And Paul tells the Thessalonians to "comfort one another with these words" about the promised resurrection of their loved ones who have recently died (1 Thessalonians 4:18).

Some verses seem to call for more than comfort; they call for encouragement. Hebrews 10:25 calls for believers "not to forsake meeting together, as is the habit of some, but to encourage each other." Paul sends Tychicus to encourage the hearts of his readers (Ephesians 6:22, Colossians 4:8).

Some verses call for a stronger form of encouragement: they call for exhortation. Paul advises Timothy not to rebuke an older man, but to "exhort him like a father" (1 Timothy 5:1). The writer of Hebrews says, "I beseech/appeal (*parakaleō*) to you, brothers/sisters, bear with my word of exhortation (*paraklēsis*)." Quite a few times both Paul and Peter "urge" or "exhort" their readers, such as in Romans 12:1: "I beseech/appeal to you therefore, brethren . . . to present your bodies as a living sacrifice," or Titus 2:6: "Likewise urge the younger men to control themselves." (See also 1 Thessalonians 5:14, 1 Timothy 1:3, 2:1, and 6:2, and 1 Peter 2:11 and 5:1, among others.)

The highest degree of urgency for *parakaleō* is the sense of imploring or begging. The servant "begged" his fellow servant to forgive the debt he owed (Matthew 18:29). The man with the legion of demons "begged" Jesus to cast them into the swine (Mark 5:12). Paul "implores" Euōdia and Syntychē to agree in the Lord (Philippians 4:2). The disciples at Lydda "beg" Peter to come when Dorcas dies (Acts 9:38). Likewise, the Jews "beg" Jesus to heal the centurion's servant (Luke 7:4). And Paul writes to the Corinthians, "We beseech you on behalf of Christ, be reconciled to God" (2 Corinthians 5:20).

But sometimes it's hard to tell how intensely to translate *parakaleō*. Does Peter "exhort" or "beg" the crowd at Pentecost to "Save yourselves from this crooked generation!" (Acts 2:40)? Your guess is as good as mine. In the Prodigal Son parable, does the father "entreat" or "beg" the older brother to come to the celebration (Luke 15:28)? How urgent are Paul's and Peter's appeals to their readers? It's hard to tell without asking them. And did Jesus have to beg, or merely encourage, God when he asks, "Do you think that I cannot appeal to my Father, and he will now provide me more than twelve legions of angels?" (Matthew 26:53).

Such a spectrum of nuances for this verb and its related nouns: from "comfort," to "encourage," to "exhort," to "beg," with options like "appeal," "beseech," "urge," and "entreat"! The beauty of it is that as you read, you can decide for yourself which translation is best, using the context of the verse, and the translation options I have given you. I "encourage" you to use what you now know about this set of words to give deeper understanding to your reading. No need to "beg" you or "beseech" you! And you can take "comfort" in the fact that in cases like *parakaleō*, there's more than one correct way to read the word!

46

Worthy, Sizeable, or Sufficient?

TO US, THERE'S QUITE a difference between saying that someone is "worthy," and saying, "Oh, they'll do." Yet the New Testament word *hikanos* (used thirty-nine times) can and does mean both of these meanings, plus it can also mean an unspecific "sizeable" number or amount. Let's see how it does that by looking at some well-known Scriptures where it does so, and compare the word to the word *axios*, which has a much clearer meaning.

In Matthew 3:11 (= Mark 1:7, Luke 3:16), John the Baptist says that he is not "worthy" to carry Jesus' sandals (John uses the word *axios* in John 1:27 and Acts 13:25). In Matthew 8:8 and Luke 7:6, the centurion at Capernaum says that he is not "worthy" to have Jesus come under his roof, while in Luke 7:4, the local Jewish elders say that the centurion *is* worthy, using the word *axios* (the centurion denies it using both words). And in 1 Corinthians 15:9, Paul says he is not "worthy" to be an apostle, because he persecuted the church of God.

A particularly prominent use of this word is in 2 Timothy 2:2, where Paul counsels Timothy to entrust Paul's teachings to faithful persons who will be "able" (or should we say "worthy" or "sufficient"?) to teach others also. Knowing all three options for this word is particularly helpful for this passage; the reader may judge for himself/herself which precise meaning fits what Paul was saying.

Another interesting use of *hikanos* is in Acts 17:9, after the anti-Christian riot in Thessalonika. The rioters accuse Paul and his partners of being anti-Caesar, which disturbs the authorities when they hear this. So in order to insure that there will be no more trouble, the authorities take *hikanos* from Jason (Paul's local host) and let Paul and his comrades go free. Our Bibles translate this as security or the like (i.e., bail). A good literal way to translate here would be "sufficiency," that is, "enough" money to guarantee that there will be no more trouble. (We could also go to the third meaning described below.)

A second, more common meaning for *hikanos* is "sufficient" or "enough." When Jesus warns his followers that after he is gone they may need a weapon or two, Peter says, "Look, Lord, here are two swords," and Jesus says, "It is enough" (Luke 22:38). Jesus may mean "enough" swords, or "enough" said; it is doubtful that he means "worthy" or "quite a few" (our next upcoming meaning).

Paul uses this word three times in 2 Corinthians. When speaking of the church's response to the serious sin of the man who married his father's wife, he says in 2:6, "Such punishment by the majority is *enough*." In verse 16 (NRSV), when talking about how God uses the church as an aroma of Christ to the world, Paul asks, "Who is *sufficient* for these things?" And in the next chapter (3:5–6), Paul says, "Not that we are *sufficient* (NRSV: *competent*) to think of anything as coming from ourselves; our *sufficiency* (or *competency*—noun form of *hikanos*) is from God, who made us *competent* (verb form of *hikanos*) to be servants of a new covenant." Again, let the reader decide what it means to be "enough" in this verse.

When the chief priests are doing damage control after Jesus rises from his tomb, we are told that they gave a "sufficient amount" (*hikanos*) of silver to pay off the guards (Matthew 28:12). This passage opens the door to the third meaning of *hikanos*: "sizeable." What do you think? Did the chief priests pay the guards simply "enough" silver, or did they pay them a "sizeable" amount? Both are possible.

Mark 10:46 tells us that a "sizeable" crowd traveled with Jesus through Jericho. Paul says that because of abuse of the Lord's Supper, a "sizeable number" have died (1 Corinthians 11:30). This third meaning of *hikanos* is a favorite way for Luke to speak in his Gospel and in Acts (he uses this meaning twenty-three times) about a "long" time (Luke 20:9) and "large" crowds (Acts 11:24) or a "pretty big" light that blinded Saul on the Damascus Road (Acts 22:6).

The Greek Old Testament gives us a sizeable added number of times *hikanos* is used. To summarize, the vast majority of the time the word is used to mean "enough" or "sufficient." In Exodus 4:10, Moses complains he is not "sufficient" to be God's spokesman. In Genesis 30:15, Leah's words in Hebrew are "Is it a small thing to you?", which in Greek becomes, "Isn't it enough for you?" Exodus 36:7 reports that the Israelites had collected "enough" material to build their portable shrine. Proverbs 30:15 lists the creatures that are never pleased to say "Enough." But the most remarkable use of *hikanos* in the Greek version of the Hebrew Bible is the four times (Job 21:15, 31:2, and 40:2, and Ruth 1:20) where "the Almighty" (Hebrew *Shaddai)* is translated as the "Sufficient One" or "Worthy One" (take your pick) rather than as *Pantokratōr* ("All-ruling").

A more precise term for "worthy" is the word *axios* (used forty-one times). John the Baptist cries, "Bear fruit *worthy* of repentance!" (Matthew 3:8 NRSV). Jesus says, "The laborer is *worthy* of his hire" (Luke 10:7). "The wedding feast is ready, but those who were called were not *worthy*" (Matthew 22:8). The Prodigal Son says, "I am no longer *worthy* to be called your son" (Luke 15:19 NRSV). The thief on the cross says, "We are receiving *things that are worthy* of what we have done" (Luke 23:41). "You are *worthy*, our Lord and God!" (Revelation 4:11 NRSV). "*Worthy* is the Lamb who was slain!" (Revelation 5:12). "You have given them blood to drink; they are *worthy*" (Revelation 16:6).

The predominant meaning of *axios* proves to be more than simply "enough," but positively meritorious or deserving. Take note: those who are guilty of the sins listed in Romans 1 (that means all of us) are "worthy" of death (Romans 1:32). But thanks be to God, "the saying is sure and *worthy* of full acceptance: that Christ Jesus came into the world to save sinners" (1 Timothy 1:15 NRSV).

47

Let Go! = Leave, Allow, or Forgive?

IMAGINE: A BIBLICAL WORD that means both "forgive," and "divorce"! How can one word mean both? Both of these actions are forms of "letting go." What an amazingly flexible word!

The standard New Testament verb for "forgive" is *aphiēmi*, used 143 times. The basic meaning of the word is to "let go away." From here, it regularly stretches to mean not only "forgive," but also "leave," "allow," and other forms of "letting go." The meaning of the word in any given verse is almost never in doubt, but we'd never guess that the same word is being stretched like Silly-Putty to cover so many different meanings, in so many famous passages. Let's take a look at a few!

The first meaning of this word for "forgive" is to "let go" or release. When Jesus dies on the cross, we are told that he "*yielded* his spirit" or "*gave up* the ghost" (Matthew 27:50). In another Gospel, Jesus "utters" a loud cry (same word—Mark 15:37).

The New Testament word for "forgive" most often (at least fifty-eight times) means to "leave" as in "go away." But it never does so without specifying a place, person, or object that is left behind. In Matthew 4:11, the devil "leaves" Jesus. Soon thereafter, his disciples "leave" their nets (Matthew 4:20). Peter says that he and his fellow disciples "have left everything" to follow Jesus (Matthew 19:27, Mark 10:28). Jesus predicts that not one stone of the Temple will be "left" that will not be thrown down (Matthew 24:2), and he predicts that there will come a day at the end of time when "one is taken, and one is left" (Matthew 24:40-41). Here also belongs the use of this verb to mean "divorce" or literally "leave" one's spouse (1 Corinthians 7:11–13).

Jesus tells a would-be follower to "leave the dead to bury their own dead" (Matthew 8:22). Jesus teaches that if someone sues you for your shirt, "leave" him your coat as well (Matthew 5:40). In the Sadducees' parable of the seven brothers, each man dies and "leaves" his wife to his brother (Matthew 22:25). On several occasions, Jesus "leaves" (some Bibles translate "sends away") the crowds (Matthew 13:36, Mark 4:36, 8:13).

Sometimes the sense of "leave" goes so far as to mean "abandon," as when the disciples leave Jesus when he is arrested (Matthew 26:56 = Mark 14:50). In his letter to the seven churches of Asia, Jesus complains, "You have left the love you had at first" (Revelation 2:4). Jesus complains that the Pharisees have "neglected" (dismissed, blown off) the weightier matters of the Law (Matthew 23:23). Paul states that men have "*abandoned* the natural use of women" and burned with lust for one another (Romans 1:27).

One unusual use of this verb with the opposite intention is in Hebrews 6:1, where readers are urged to "leave behind" the elemental teachings of Christ and move forward toward maturity or perfection. Here, the idea is not to forsake the basic teachings of the Christian message, but to make progress, not to leave them behind or abandon them.

A few times, this word for "forgive" is used to mean "leave alone." Jesus responds to the claim that Mary has wasted three hundred denarii worth of ointment on Jesus by saying, "Leave her (alone)" (John 12:7). Jesus responds to a complaint from the Pharisees by saying, "Leave them (alone)—they are blind guides" (Matthew 15:14). When Jesus cries out from thirst on the cross, the crowds say, "Leave him (alone); let's see if Elijah will come to save him" (Matthew 27:49).

One more major meaning of this word used for "forgive" is to "allow." Jesus tells John to "allow" him to be baptized, so John "allowed" it (Matthew 3:15). "*Allow* me to take that speck out of your eye" (Matthew 7:4). "*Let* the little children come to me" (Matthew 19:14). Jesus "would not *permit* the demons to speak" (Mark 1:34 NRSV). Jesus also complains that the Pharisees will not enter the Kingdom, "nor do you *allow* to enter those who want to enter" (Matthew 23:13). And in his letters to the churches of Asia, Jesus' chief complaint against Thyatira (Revelation 2:20) is that "You allow (in our twenty-first-century idiom, we would say "tolerate") the woman Jezebel." (Certainly there is a warning here to today's churches not to be too tolerant, like Thyatira was.)

LET GO! = LEAVE, ALLOW, OR FORGIVE?

But forty-nine times, this word *aphiēmi* means "forgive." It is the verb used in the Lord's Prayer: "Forgive us our debts, as we also have forgiven our debtors" (Matthew 6:12 NRSV). It is the same verb used in Jesus' command to forgive 490 times, and in the parable of the Unforgiving Servant (Matthew 18:21–35). In his teaching on forgiveness, Jesus comes dangerously close to making salvation conditional on us forgiving everyone who has ever wronged us, although I believe that is a misunderstanding of his intent.

(The other verb for "forgive," *charizomai*, is used twelve times in the New Testament, such as in Colossians 2:13. It means to literally "exercise grace" toward someone, to treat them with undeserved favor. Much of the time, forgiveness does mean showing kindness to those who do not deserve it, like God does to us.)

Jesus' teaching on forgiveness was by far the most radical of any ancient teaching on the subject. His teaching on forgiveness is historical bedrock that would never have been invented by pretenders. Who would invent a Jesus who makes it so hard to faithfully follow him?

Yes, I look for excuses not to do what Jesus says. I jokingly say that if we take Jesus strictly literally, we're off the hook after we've forgiven 490 times (which would only take one week on some of our nastier freeways). Or I can say that if my opponents show me the wrong kind of love in the way they treat me, I can triple their "love" back! But I cannot honestly dismiss Jesus' teaching this way. I know he's right, and I know his teaching is for my own good. By failing to forgive, we are only hurting ourselves. Forgiveness cuts the nerve to end the vicious cycle of vengeance. Forgiveness is possibly the greatest way we "let go" of what's killing us deep inside. To echo a former radio host, "Don't let your enemies live rent-free in your head."

Beyond forgiveness, what other forms of "letting go" do we need to do? We need to let go of the past; we can echo what was good from the past, but we cannot go back there, nor should we try, and if there was pain in our past, so much more reason to let go of it. We need to let go of possessions that actually possess us. We need to let go of our resentments and unreasonable expectations from life. Ultimately, we need to let go of self and our need to control. There's plenty to let go of!

Aphiēmi is an amazingly versatile word! Thankfully, its basic meanings are in little doubt in any given passage, but readers are free to take these meanings "leave," "allow," and "forgive" and use them to give added color to our reading of God's word.

48

Authority: The Power or Right to Act

THE WORD "AUTHORITY" (GREEK word *exousia*) is found 102 times in the New Testament. Bauer's lexicon summarizes the uses of *exousia* into the following categories. The first category is freedom of choice, the right to act or decide. We find this meaning in John 10:18, where Jesus says, "I have the right/authority to lay down (my life), and I have the right/authority to take it up again." The second category is ability, capability, might, or power. The two prophets in Revelation 11:6 have the ability (obviously given to them by God) to stop the rain, to turn the waters into blood, and strike the earth with any plague.

The third meaning of this word is authority or absolute power to give orders. The devil says to Jesus in Luke 4:6 that he will give power over the whole world to Jesus, "because it has been handed over to me, and I give it to whomever I wish." The fourth and final meaning of this word is the ruling powers themselves, both human and cosmic, people or spirits who are in a position to command. Paul says in 1 Corinthians 15:24 that one day Christ will abolish every ruler and authority and power.

What kind of authority was given to the priesthood in God's word? The answer is: very little. We don't find the subject at all in the New Testament. In the Hebrew Bible, priests are given authority to declare people clean or unclean, to assess the value of people and property, and offer sacrifices on behalf of worshippers. They also had the responsibility to teach God's law, but here, their authority was entirely dependent on God's revealed written word.

AUTHORITY: THE POWER OR RIGHT TO ACT

The Gospels tell us that Jesus grabs attention immediately when he begins to preach, because he spoke "like one having authority" (Matthew 7:29 = Mark 1:22 = Luke 4:32). He didn't speak like the rabbis, who quoted long lists of "Rabbi So-and-So said" citations to back up their teaching. He was able to speak on his word alone, and people knew that it was from God. Jesus could say, "But I say to you," and people knew it was far more than his personal opinion.

Jesus grabs more attention when he claims and proves to have the "authority" to forgive sins, a department that ultimately belonged to God alone (Matthew 9:6 = Mark 2:10). While some sins are also wrongs done against fellow humans who have the option to forgive the wrongs done to them, only God is in a position to forgive all wrongdoing. We humans have no right or authority to announce the forgiveness of anyone's sins against God, except on the basis of what God has done through the cross of Jesus Christ, as proclaimed in God's word.

Jesus shares with the Twelve the authority to cast out demons and to heal, meaning, the power to speak and make it happen (Matthew 10:1 = Luke 9:1). Here is one place where we find ourselves totally dependent on God. Even Simon the sorcerer knew he did not have the channel to God that the apostles had, and he found that not even money could buy that power.

After Jesus cleanses the Temple, the Jerusalem leaders demand to know by what "authority" Jesus acts and speaks (Matthew 21:23–27 = Mark 11:28–33). Why should we listen to you? Who backs you up? Jesus counters by asking where John the Baptist's authority came from, a question they are afraid to answer. The leaders seem to know that John and Jesus get their authority from the same place, an authority that they don't have, even though they occupy the offices where that authority ought to reside.

Pilate thought he had authority over Jesus: "Do you not know that I have the authority to release you, and the authority to crucify you?" But Jesus reminds Pilate that he has no authority except what was given him from above (John 19:10–11).

At the end of his earthly ministry, Jesus makes it clear that he commands far more authority than his earthly audience ever could have fathomed up till then: "All authority in heaven and on earth has been given unto me" (Matthew 28:18). The fact that he commands such authority gives us the grounds for his Great Commission: "Go there and make disciples of all nations, baptizing them in the name of the Father, and of the Son, and of the Holy Spirit, teaching them to observe all that I have commanded you."

Some authority will never be delegated. God has fixed times and seasons by his own authority (Acts 1:7). Jesus says he has the "authority" to judge the world (John 5:27). Only God has the "authority" (*or* power) to cast people into Gehenna/Hell (Luke 12:5). And while we are told that God allows the powers of evil to exercise some measure of authority here and there, God also reserves the option to shut that authority down at any time.

In Luke 22:53, Jesus surrenders to the "*power* of darkness" to allow him to be arrested. In Revelation 13:2, the beast gets the power of the dragon and his throne and "great *authority*." But Paul says in Acts 26:18 that his job is to turn people "from the *authority* of Satan to God." Colossians 1:13 says that God has "rescued us from the authority/power of darkness, and has transferred us into the kingdom of his beloved Son."

Paul compares God to the potter who has the authority (= sovereign right) to do with the clay whatever he chooses (Romans 9:21). Not everybody believes that. A lot of folks seem to think they can sit in judgment over God and dictate to God what is fair and not fair. Must God give us all equal breaks in life, equal goods, and/or equal talents? Jesus' Parable of the Talents proves otherwise. The truth is that God owes us nothing. God has the indisputable right to do as God chooses, within God's own self-imposed laws.

So what authority has God given to us? John writes in John 1:12 that to as many as received Christ, to them he gave the authority (authorization?) to become children of God. (Notice that none of us were children of God before we received that authorization.) God has given authority to leaders like Peter (Matthew 16:19), Paul (2 Corinthians 10:8), and Titus (Titus 2:15—the word used here is the less common *epitagē*). And God appears to have given to a select few today the power to heal and/or to cast out evil spirits, although such persons must each be judged by their fruits, as to whether their power comes from God or from another source.

But the only authority given to believers at large, both men and women, is based entirely on our faithfulness to God's word in what we proclaim and practice. No one has been given a trump card to say, "I am right and you are wrong, because I have the authority to speak and act for God." Our authority stands or falls entirely on our faithfulness to what God says, which listeners must judge for themselves. Authority cannot be claimed; it must be earned. And God gives us no signed certificates to prove to whom God has given authority.

AUTHORITY: THE POWER OR RIGHT TO ACT

What about the "keys of the kingdom of heaven" that Jesus gives to Peter in Matthew 16:19? Jesus tells Peter that whatever he binds (or forbids) on earth shall be bound in heaven, and whatever he (literally) "looses" (= permits) on earth shall be "loosed" in heaven. The question is whether Peter is being given the authority of a Pope or divine spokesman. No, it is much more likely that Jesus is simply highlighting Peter's office as an apostle, giving him the power of attorney to make decisions based on Jesus' teaching, wherever Jesus did not explicitly address an issue of faith or practice. Jesus never mentioned abortion or child molestation by name, but by the end of the first century, the early church had the authoritative answers on those issues, most likely based on the unwritten teachings of Peter and his fellow apostles.

But there is no evidence that Jesus intended that authority to bind and loose to extend beyond Peter's lifetime, nor is there evidence that Jesus intended that authority to be passed on to anyone else. Indeed, when the early church confronted the biggest issue to which Jesus never spelled out his answer (namely, whether Gentiles had to be circumcised to follow Jesus), Peter does not decide the issue. It is decided by an all-church council of apostles and elders. And the whole reason they had to hold this council is that in Galatians 2:14, Paul has to rebuke Peter for getting it wrong on this very issue.

Human say-so only goes so far. Anyone can make claims about God or about truth. Philosophers can speculate and use logic. Science can make its claims, but even science must often begin with starting points that it cannot prove, that have to be accepted on faith. And today, science has sadly been hijacked by political agendas that undermine its credibility. Ultimately, there is much for which we have to rely on the revealed word of God for our authority.

Both authority and human rights are wrapped up in this word *exousia*. America was the first nation since God's word was published who spelled it out that human rights come from God, not from human government. God may delegate authority to human government, as we find in Romans 13:1, where Paul says "there is no authority except from God, and those [authorities] that exist have been appointed by God." But because God is the source of that authority, God can always take it away. Consequently, when we speak of human rights, if we claim that our rights come from government, government can take them away. But if human rights come from God, then only God has the right or authority to take them away.

49

Sorcery, or Use of Drugs?

THE WORD *PHARMAKEIA* IS the word from which we get our word "pharmacy." It is one of the sins on Paul's list of the "works of the flesh" in Galatians 5:20, and for which Babylon the Great is condemned in Revelation 18:23, as well as the list of serious sins from which apocalyptic plague victims refuse to repent (Revelation 9:21). *Pharmakeia* also appears on three of the earliest sin lists from the early church: *Didachē* 2:2 and 5:1, and *Barnabas* 20:1, while the people who practice it (*pharmakoi*) are excluded from the Holy City in Revelation 21:8 and 22:15.

Whatever it is, *pharmakeia* sounds like a moral felony that we certainly want to know more about, since Paul warns, "Those who do such things shall not inherit the kingdom of God." Could *pharmakeia* in Galatians 5:20 be biblical grounds to forbid the use of mind-altering drugs? If not, then what exactly is this sin? Let's take a closer look at this word!

In pagan Greek literature, *pharmakeia* is the use of *pharmaka*, "drugs," "potions," or "poisons." The verb *pharmakoō* means "to medicate." However, in Jewish literature, *pharmakeia* is almost always translated "sorcery" or "witchcraft." In the Greek Old Testament, the word *pharmaka* translates the Hebrew *keshaphīm* for the "sorceries" of Jezebel in 2 Kings 9:22 and the *lehaṭīm* or "secret arts" in Exodus 7:11, 7:22, 8:3, and 8:14, while *pharmakoi* is used for the Egyptian magicians in Exodus 7:11, and *pharmakeia* is used for Babylonian sorcery in Isaiah 47:9 and 47:12.

But *pharmakeia* was not the only word available for sorcery or witchcraft. There was also *mageia*, "magic" (the Magi as a social class were commonly thought of as "magicians"). Indeed, *mageia* is listed right next to *pharmakeia* on the sin lists in the *Didachē* and *Barnabas*, and *magoi* appear right next to the *pharmakoi* in the Greek version of Daniel 2:2. Perhaps we can see the *magoi* as specialists in divination, while the *pharmakoi* practiced witchcraft with a chemistry set.

The use of *pharmakeia* (drugs or potions) was not always viewed negatively. Sirach 6:16 says, "A faithful friend is a *pharmakon* of life." *Testament of Joseph* 2:7 says, "Patience is a great *pharmakon*." Ignatius (Ephesians 20:1) calls the bread of the Eucharist the "medicine of immortality." Sirach 38:4 says that "The Lord has created medicines (*pharmaka*) out of the earth, and a sensible man will not despise them." Even the Jewish philosopher Philo (*Sacrifices* 1:70–71) backhandedly concedes that drugs can be used for healing, but he thinks that people wrongfully resort to drugs instead of to God.

Drugs were sometimes used for persuasion. In *Testament of Reuben* 4:9, we are told that Potiphar's wife "summoned magicians and brought drugs (*pharmaka*)" to try to persuade Joseph to sleep with her. The historian Josephus tells us that Cleopatra tried to persuade Marc Antony to do her bidding, not only with conversation, but also with *pharmaka* (*Antiquities* 15:93), while at the same time she used a *pharmakon* to murder her brother (15:89).

There's where the potential evil of *pharmakeia* lay in the mind of most Greeks and Romans: the risk of being secretly poisoned by an enemy (like the fear of fentanyl today). *Pharmakeia* (Latin *veneficium*) was a capital crime, whether it involved poisoning victims, or any messing around with the powers of the underworld. Yet *pharmakeia* reached all the way up to Caesar's palace. Rest assured, a Roman court could tell the difference between the use of *pharmaka* by a doctor to bring healing, and the use of poisons to murder unsuspecting victims.

Opium and *kannabis* would have been the two mind-altering *pharmaka* that were best known to the biblical world. I have written more about this in chapter 5 of my first book, *What's on God's Sin List for Today?* Whether Paul and John had witchcraft, poisoning, or the abuse of drugs in mind when they used the term *pharmakeia* on their sin lists is hard to say; we do well to avoid all three. Within the central root meaning of *pharmakeia* and its related words, I see a huge potential connection between drugs and the occult. But let me share with you what I see to be the biblical basis against the use of mind-altering drugs.

First, there is Paul's teaching "Do not be drunk with wine" (Ephesians 5:18), which we discussed in chapter 5 of this book. Paul is not singling out wine, as if it were OK to be drunk with beer, liquor, marijuana, or other mind-altering drugs. No, Paul is forbidding the use of any mind-altering substance to get high. Notice that Paul contrasts drunkenness with being controlled by the Holy Spirit. We endanger ourselves any time we open our minds to forces that are not from God. Doing so is akin to witchcraft, which is why the word *pharmakeia* might fit well as a term for the dangers of abusing mind-altering drugs.

Second, we have the example of Jesus on the cross. In Matthew 27:34, Jesus was offered pain-killer ("gall") mixed with wine, which may have been either opium or absinthe, although Mark 15:23 says it was "myrrh." Whichever pain-killer he was offered, Jesus refused to endure the pain of hell for a world full of sinners while being drugged out of his mind. Yes, there is a place for the legitimate use of drugs to kill physical pain (Proverbs 31:6–7 hints at this), but we must avoid drugs as an escape from the emotional pain of life.

Which leads to the final part of our biblical basis against the abuse of drugs: 1 Corinthians 6:12, "I will not be enslaved by anything." This teaching can be applied to any addictive substance, including alcohol and tobacco, to drugs that needlessly alter our consciousness, and even good gifts of God such as food and sex. God wants to set us free from all that enslaves us!

50

R-Rated Prophets

EZEKIEL WAS LITERALLY AN R-rated prophet. St. Jerome writes to Bishop Paulinus in Epistle 53:8 that Jews in AD 400 would not let men read parts of Ezekiel until they were thirty years old, particularly the opening vision of the chariots. Similarly, the Mishnah (AD 200) states that Ezekiel 1 is restricted to be read privately, and can only be discussed one-on-one by experts (m. Ḥagigah 2:1). The Mishnah also states that both chapters 1 and 16 of Ezekiel must not be read out loud to an audience (m. *Megillah* 4:10).

Why the restrictions, you ask? The chapters about the chariot visions were withheld simply because they sounded bizarre even to ancient ears; to us, they sound like UFO's. The vision of the new Temple (Ezekiel 40–48) contains details that were hard to reconcile with the Law of Moses. But the most obvious reason to restrict the reading of Ezekiel is the very "adult" sexual rhetoric he uses. Although I will try my best to handle the subject with care, ultimately the uncensored Ezekiel is not for the squeamish. As Professor Doug Stuart told us at seminary, some of Ezekiel is not the kind of stuff you'd use in a children's sermon.

Such material is concentrated in Ezekiel 16 and 23, where Judah is portrayed as a nymphomaniac, insatiable in her desire for lovers outside of her commitment to the one true God. In Ezekiel 16:25, where God says to the nation, "You offered yourself to all passers-by," the Hebrew says literally, "You spread your legs." In 16:31, where we are told that the nation builds herself an idol shrine or platform, the Latin version says she builds herself a *lupanar* (= Greek version's *porneion* = English "brothel").

Ezekiel 16:26 uses the Hebrew expression "great of flesh" as a euphemism for a man's "package" (to use an English language euphemism). In the same passage, Ezekiel 16:17 speaks of male images of metal "with which you played the harlot." (Only recently in our age of technological advances would a meaning other than idolatry come to mind.)

Ezekiel 23:20 is about as R-rated a verse as you can get: "You taʿugabah ("sexually desired," a rare word) your concubines, whose flesh (see previous paragraph) is like the flesh of donkeys, and whose (literally "what-comes-out") is like that of horses." How graphic can the prophet get? By the way, here is the only place in the Hebrew Bible (or anywhere?) where the Hebrew word for "concubine" is used for males instead of women. Here the word appears to mean "paramours" or "boy toys."

Ezekiel, Jeremiah, and Hosea are the only authors in our canonical Bible where the Greek version uses the word *erastai*, a word that comes from the noun *erōs* ("erotic" desire), which means "lovers" in an exclusively sexual sense.

Not to be outdone, Jeremiah likens Judah to a lust-filled she-camel, "in her heat sniffing the wind. Who can restrain her lust? None who seek her need weary themselves; in her month they will find her" (Jeremiah 2:23–24 NRSV). God asks Judah in Jeremiah 3:2, "Where have you not been ——-ed?" (I suggest a verb that rhymes with "rude.") The verb used here (*shiggēl*) was considered obscene by later copyists, who directed readers in their footnotes to read the verb "laid" instead.

By comparison, Hosea's real-life soap opera, where God commands him to marry a harlot and buy her back again from sex-slavery, sounds downright tame. The term *erastai* is used five times in Hosea 2, but the rampant illicit sex practices in the Baʿal worship that Hosea condemns make the term entirely appropriate.

Why did God speak in such shocking terms? The question presumes (correctly, I would say) that God actually inspired these words, and that we should not blame the prophets themselves for them. Perhaps God found it necessary to use such images and language to get the attention of an unshockable people.

But God does not speak this way all the time. Referring to the wild ways of the surrounding Gentile world, Paul writes, "It is shameful even to speak of the things they do in secret" (Ephesians 5:12). When I taught Latin at a classical Christian college, I would steer my students away from reading the comic poet Martial, because his material was definitely R-rated, if not worse. Paul knows the Roman world around him is far beyond R-rated.

In the cases of both Paul and the Hebrew prophets, audience was everything. Paul's Greco-Roman audience needed no details on the depravity around them; they needed to flush it out of their lips, eyes, ears, and minds. By contrast, the audience of the Hebrew prophets could not see their own depravity, until it was portrayed for them in shockingly graphic form.

The R-rated portions of the prophets are few, but even without them, the Bible is not a children's book. Yet the Bible is not pornographic. It is frank, but it is not designed to feed the twisted parts of our natures. It is written to convince us, in sometimes graphic detail, of how much we need a Savior.

51

Russia and China: Major Players in the Last Days?

WILL RUSSIA AND CHINA play a major role in the final days of human history? Will they hijack or try to influence the outcome of what God plans to do? The evidence is debatable, but a convincing case can be made that they will. There is much more evidence concerning Russia than what we could say for China in the Bible. Let's take a look at the evidence.

Magog is found only in Genesis 10, 1 Chronicles 1, and Revelation 20. Magog may have appeared on the Hebrew radar screen as *mat-Gagayya*, a nation mentioned in the Amarna Letters around 1400 BC. Josephus says they are the Scythians of ancient Russia. Ambrose (AD 200s) claims that Gog and Magog are the Goths. Gog has been linked by some to Gugu, leader of Lydia (western Turkey) in the time of Ezekiel, but that may be merely appearance; certainly this Gog did none of what Ezekiel predicted. Curiously, in Numbers 24:7, the Septuagint reads "Gog" for "Agag."

What about Rōsh? Ezekiel 38:2 reads either "*head/chief* prince of Meshech and Tubal" *or* "prince of *Rōsh*, Meshech, and Tubal." An article by James Price entitled "Rosh: An Ancient Land Known to Ezekiel" (see bibliography) argues that *rōsh* cannot be an adjective because it would interrupt a possessive chain. It can be counter-argued that *rōsh* cannot be part of a list of three countries because there is no Hebrew word "and" in front of Meshech, but Ezekiel violates this grammatical rule twice in this section.

The Septuagint reads the word in question as *Rōs*, a name that is subsequently applied to the whole region north of the Black Sea. It is objected that modern Russia first appears in the AD 800s, but it is obvious that the place name seems to have long pre-dated the existence of the people. Jon Marc Ruthven (*The Prophecy That Is Shaping History*—see bibliography), the most scholarly defender of Russia in end-times prophecy, documents all of the above evidence, plus he identifies a number of ancient territories northeast and northwest of Assyria with the name *Ras*.

What about Meshech and Tubal? Contrary to Hal Lindsey and his sources, these are not Moscow and Tobolsk! Both are states in eastern Turkey (Mushki and Tabal) known to the Assyrians in the 700s BC. In fact, Mushki was ruled at this time by the fabled king Midas (*Mita*). Scratch these two names from the list of references to Russia, but not from its list of potential allies.

Gomer and all his hordes were known to the Assyrians as *Gimirayya*, their name for the Cimmerians or Scythians, whom Homer says live near the entrance to Hades in "one long melancholy night." One of the sons of Gomer in Genesis 10/1 Chronicles 1 is Ashkenaz (Assyrian *Iškuza*), another name for the Scythians, although Jews have long used "Ashkenazi" as a term for German/Eastern European Jews (similarly, Josephus locates the sons of Ashkenaz in the area of the Danube).

So Gog and Magog, Rosh, and Gomer could all be part of the "Russian Federation" envisioned by Ezekiel in chapters 38–39 that invades Israel in the latter days. Their allies include Persia (= modern Iran), Cush (= Nubia, in modern Sudan), Put (= Egyptian name for Libya), and nations from the area of modern Turkey, including Meshech, Tubal, and Togarmah (named after the ancient Hittite city Tegarama).

Russia, Iran, Turkey, Sudan, and Libya—an eerily modern-looking scenario! Opposing this apparent end-times coalition, Ezekiel names Sheba and Dedan (both located on the Arabian peninsula; Sheba = Yemen), Tarshish (located in Spain or Tunisia), and the "Coastlands" (*'iyyim*), encompassing the Greek islands, western Europe, and possibly even the Americas (although it is doubtful that the Americas were known to the Hebrews).

The strongest candidate for a biblical reference to China is Isaiah 49:12, a description of Jews returning from captivity: "Behold, these shall come from far away, and behold, these from the north and from the west, and these from the land of Sinim." While eminent scholars including Gesenius and Delitzsch seriously believed this to be a reference to China, others in the past two centuries have emended the text from *synym* to *swnym*, which would mean "Aswan" or "Syene" in far southern Egypt. The

Dead Sea Scrolls (1QIsa) contain such a reading, although even there it may be an attempted correction rather than an original reading; it may be that the Dead Sea copyists preferred a familiar place name to a name they knew nothing of. The Latin version reads *de terra australi*, "from the land of the south" (not Australia, although it is amusing to consider!). The Greek version reads "from the land of the Persians," which may be a directional stab in the dark, or a directional understatement; the land in question may be much further east than Persia.

Sinae is the Latin name for the Qin (Ch'in) state, founded in approximately the ninth or eighth century BC, although the Romans and Greeks usually referred to China as "Silk-Land" (*Serica*). So *Sinim* as a potential reference to the land which became China, by the name by which it became known, is plausible for the writer of this scripture, whether it was written by Isaiah ben-Amoz (690 BC?) or by a later writer (540 BC?). However, if this is a reference to the early Qin state, it is the only one we can find in the ancient Near East; any other such references must be under a name hitherto never associated with the Far East.

The only other possible reference to the Chinese is in Revelation 16:12, the "kings from the East" who come in the final days before the return of Christ from beyond the Euphrates, for whom we are given their number: 200 million of them (Revelation 9:16). It is a number probably larger than the entire population of the planet in AD 95, but it has been argued that today's China could potentially field an army that large. The claim that this is China cannot be proved, but neither can it be easily dismissed.

But while China may have been barely if at all visible on the radar of the biblical audience, China was always important to God. It is fascinating to trace the evidence of the Gospel's arrival in China. Leading the way was a Nestorian bishop named Alopen in AD 635, who composed the first Christian writing in Chinese, *The Sutra of Jesus the Messiah*. As defective as the Nestorian understanding of Christ may have been (a schizophrenic juxtaposition of divine and human natures), it was apparently good enough for God to use anyway. Syrian Orthodox missionaries came soon thereafter. The Xian-Fu stone (AD 781), inscribed in both Chinese and Syriac, contains the names of over seventy Christian leaders in China.

Who would have dreamed how God's church in China would have exploded with growth since 1949? It has been jokingly observed that Mao Zedong was one of the greatest evangelists who ever lived, because he bulldozed obstacles to the Gospel that might have taken decades to overcome.

Mao built roads, imposed a single language, made the nation literate, swept away the old gods and goddesses, and created a spiritual vacuum that only Christ could fill. Praise God for today's huge army of our Chinese sisters and brothers in Christ, an army so big that it would have staggered the minds of anyone from biblical times! Indeed, the only one who ever saw that huge crowd of Chinese believers was John (Revelation 7:9), and even he was unable to name them by name.

Do we have a road map for exactly who will do what at the end of the world? Even if we think that all of these players have been positively identified (which we cannot do), we still have no clue as to when it will happen. We cannot equate the end-times players named in the Bible to today's Russia or Iran or China. See how much the political map of Central Asia has changed in the past thirty years! Enmities and alliances morph back and forth. Still, I am convinced that Ezekiel's prophecy will come true, not as non-literal symbols of a heavenly war, but as events that can be located on whatever earthly map exists at the time when it happens.

It appears that Russia and China will play a major role in trying to influence the outcome of this final conflict. But how exactly the world will end militarily or politically is not our concern as believers. Jesus has charged us to target Russia and China as two of the many nations from whom we are to make disciples. As we seek to influence the outcome of the lives of souls who do not yet know Christ and who stand to be lost eternally without him, Jesus assures us that the gates of Hades will not prevail in our efforts.

52

Anti Ain't the Word We Thought It Was

ANTI MEANS "AGAINST," DOESN'T it? Not in Greek, even though that's where we got the word from. Perhaps I overstate a bit, but the word *anti* means "against" in English far more than it does in Greek. Examining the uses of this word gives us a rich picture of meaning that can illuminate some key passages of God's word, including the very heart of our message of the cross.

While the word *anti* is used only seventeen times in the Greek New Testament, it is used 170 times in the Septuagint, and there it consistently means "in place of" or "instead of," from which by extension we get the notion of "against" or "opposed to," although sometimes it means "in exchange for." A tour through the Septuagint is in order here.

In Genesis 9:6, God says, "Whoever sheds the blood of man, *in exchange for* his blood it shall be shed." Also, in Genesis 4:25 we read, "God has raised up for me another seed *in place of* Abel." Here, *anti* cannot mean "against," because Seth and Abel cannot be construed to be against each other. In Joel 4:3, Israel's enemies have sold a girl "*in exchange for/for the price of* wine." In Psalm 109:4–5, the writer complains about his enemies: "*In exchange* for my love, they are my accusers . . . They reward me evil *in exchange for* good, and hatred *in exchange for* my love." Proverbs 17:13 likewise warns that evil will not depart from those who reward "evil *in exchange for* good." Zephaniah 2:10 reads, "This they shall have *for/in place of/because of* their pride." In Hebrews 12:16, Esau sells his birthright "at the price of" a single meal.

Anti is used six times in quotes where the biblical writer condemns the returning of "evil *for* evil." It is also used sixteen times in the three Mosaic Law passages that record the law of retaliation ("an eye *for* an eye" and other examples). Exodus 21 gives six more instances where payment must be made "in exchange for" (*anti*) damages done.

The phrase *ant' autou* (= *anti autou*, "in his stead/place") is used eighty-four times in the Septuagint, particularly when kings die and their replacements begin to reign. In the New Testament, we find this use only where Archelaus rules "in place of" Herod (Matthew 2:22).

The phrase *anth' ōn* (= *anti-hōn*, "because of these things") is used 108 times in the Septuagint. Both Psalm 109:16 and Jeremiah 5:19 answer the question, "Because of what has YHWH done all these things?" We also find this use of *anti* in Jeremiah 27:7 (LXX = Hebrew and English 50:7), and Ezekiel 25:3 and 25:6.

Ephesians 5:31 gives us a novel use of this word in its quote of Genesis 2:22: "*For this reason*, a man shall leave his father and mother." Paul's version of this text is not found in the Septuagint, or in Jesus' quotes in Matthew 19:5 and Mark 10:7! In these texts, a different Greek expression is used. Since Paul does not seem to be citing anything he has written in his preceding verse, he appears to be making his own independent translation, using *anti toutou* ("Because of this") as a variation of the above expression that was used in Psalm 109:16 and eighty-three other times.

Luke 11:11 asks, How many parents will pull a bait-and-switch on their child, and give them a snake "instead" of a fish when asked? In 1 Corinthians 11:15, Paul declares that a woman's hair is given to her "instead" or "in place of" a head covering. James 4:15 warns readers who make too many plans they may not live to see, "*instead of* you saying, if the Lord wills, we shall live and do this or that." In Ezekiel 4:15, when God commands the prophet to bake his bread on dung, God allows him to use "cow's dung *instead of* human dung."

John 1:16 is a real puzzler: "From his fullness have we all received grace *anti* grace." The picture seems to be God's undeserved favor being dumped on us in buckets, with one bucket being rapidly swapped out for another. "Grace upon grace" (NRSV) or "one gracious blessing after another" (NLT) is the best we can do in our translations.

The word "Antichrist" is found nowhere in Jewish or pagan Greek, and is found in the New Testament only in 1 John 2:18, 2:22, and 4:3, and 2 John 1:7. While we tend to think of this figure as "against" or "opposing" Christ, one might argue based on what I have observed above that this character comes "in place of" or "instead of" Christ. The "against" meaning for *anti* that we know so well in English *can* be found in compounds such as *antagonizomai* (struggle against), *antilegō* (speak against), and *antithesis* (counter-proposal). The word *antigraphon* (Mark 16:9, title for the shorter ending) means a replacement text.

All that we have said about the word *anti* illuminates two of the most profound passages of Scripture. The first is Jesus' words found in Matthew 20:28 (= Mark 10:45) that the Son of Man came "to give his life as a ransom in exchange for/in place of (*anti*) many." (A similar use is found in Matthew 17:27, where Jesus instructs Peter to take the coin he finds in the fish's mouth and give it to the collectors of the Temple tax "*on behalf of* you and me.")

The other passage is Hebrews 12:2, which tells us that Jesus, "*in exchange for* (or is it *instead of*?) the joy set before him, endured the cross." A case can be made for "instead of," based on the root meaning of *anti*, which would mean that Jesus turned down a chance for his own personal joy in order to endure the cross. But "in exchange for" is much more likely. Jesus endured the pain of the cross, "in exchange for" the joy of setting a countless crowd of sinners free from sin and eternal death.

Anti ain't the word we thought it was, was it? "Against" doesn't begin to do justice to its meaning. The meaning of *anti* makes a huge difference as we meditate on how Jesus took our place in his saving death on the cross.

53

God Is *"Hyper"* about Us!

"If God is for us, who can be against us?" "Who (or what) shall separate us from the love of Christ?" What wonderful questions! What wonderful answers: No one and nothing! God's bottom line is: if Jesus Christ has taken away our sin, then nothing can stand in the way between us and God. Here in the last nine verses of Romans chapter 8, we will see that God is literally "hyper" about us!

Paul asks, "Who shall bring any charge against God's chosen ones?" Who's got the legal ammunition that can wrench us away from God and cast us into the pit of hell? God is the One who declares us not guilty. Who's the innocent party who has the legal standing to point the accusing finger at us? Only Jesus Christ, and he's the One who died to put us right with God, who rose from the dead to clear our way to God, and who at this moment continues to plead for us at the throne of God. *He's* going to accuse us? I don't think so! In the person of Jesus Christ, God has suffered all the pain of hell in our place, so that God can embrace us as beloved children, so that we may be reconciled and reunited with the One who loves us more than words can say.

What else can stand in the way between God and God's children? Can some evil power drive a wedge between us, or steal us away from the arms of God? Is there anyone powerful enough to out-wrestle God for our souls? Is there some Incredible Hulk out there who's going to step in and say, "Get lost, buster! He's mine! She's mine!"? Is there some future event in our lives, some scandal, some horrible mistake, that's going to tear us away from God? Can any death we could die turn God against us?

Can altitude or geography separate us from God? Is there a windswept peak, or some dark ocean trench, that is literally God-forsaken? Is there any planet in space where we can say that we are no longer in God's grasp? Paul's answer is a resounding "No!"

All that's left that can possibly alienate us from God is the bitter circumstances of life, and what they may do to us from within. Pressure, anxiety, harassment, starvation, not having a thread to wear, danger, lethal weapons pointed straight at us—Paul writes that none of these can stand between God and us, but they all have the potential to erect huge barriers in our hearts toward God, to turn us away from God. Only an inside job can do that.

"If God is for us, who can be against us?" The word Paul uses to mean "for" us is the word "*hyper*." Here it means "in our place". It also means "over the top" (which is what we mean when we say "hyper-active" or "hyper-sensitive").

The word *hyper* is used 132 times in the New Testament, twenty-eight times in 2 Corinthians alone. Twelve times it is used in a geometrical sense ("above"—Matthew 10:24, 1 Corinthians 10:13), plus five times in the figurative sense "beyond" or "more than" (2 Corinthians 11:23). But it is used 115 times to mean "for" or "on behalf of," including twenty-three times to speak of praying "for/on behalf of" someone. Jesus says in Mark 9:40 NRSV (= Luke 9:50), "Whoever is not against us is *for* us," i. e., they're on our side.

Hyper can be used to speak of someone risking their life "for/on behalf of" someone (such as in Romans 16:4), suffering for/on behalf of someone (2 Corinthians 1:6), boasting for/on behalf of someone (2 Corinthians 12:5), or serving on someone's behalf (Colossians 1:7). It is also the word used for offering sacrifices "on behalf of" someone (such as in Hebrews 5:1). This includes the greatest sacrifice, to die on behalf of someone, to lay down one's life "for/on behalf of" one's friends (John 15:13).

Twenty-six times we are told that God Incarnate did this for us. Jesus told us he would do this at the Last Supper (Mark 14:24, Luke 22:19–20, 1 Corinthians 11:24—see also John 6:51). Paul tells us twice in Romans 5:6–8 that Christ died "*on behalf of* the ungodly . . . while we were still his enemies." Paul tells us in 1 Corinthians 15:3 that one of *the* most important parts of his Gospel was that "Christ died *for* our sins." Want more? See John 10:11–15, Romans 14:15, 2 Corinthians 5:14–15, Galatians 1:4, 2:20, and

3:13, Ephesians 5:2 and 5:25, 1 Thessalonians 5:10, 1 Timothy 2:6, Titus 2:14, Hebrews 10:12, 1 Peter 2:21 and 3:18, and 1 John 3:16.

Why do I belabor this point? Because today there are many voices out there that question and/or deny the substitutionary atonement of Christ. To do so, we must either close our eyes to all of these passages, or chop them out of our Bible. No, the truth that Jesus died on our behalf, as our substitute, is absolutely central to the Good News we proclaim to the world. Here in the cross of Jesus Christ and all that he has done for us, we see that God is literally "hyper" about us!

When we take a quick look at Romans 8:31-39, we find the word "hyper" four times. Verse 31: "If God is *hyper* us" (if God going to bat for us in our place), "who can be against us?" Verse 32: God "gave up his Son *hyper* us" (in our exchange). Verse 34: Christ is at the right hand of God, "pleading *hyper* us" (on our behalf).

All these meanings would come to mind for Paul's audience when they heard the word *"hyper"* used to describe God's attitude toward us. God is *hyper* about us! That doesn't mean that God's whole being revolves around us, as if God existed just for us. It does mean that God is on our side, that God has gone over the top for us. It does mean that God has gone to bat in our place, that he has suffered the pain of hell so that we would never have to do so. It does mean that God is pulling for us when we're down. It does mean that God is our greatest fan. God's love goes "over the top" for us!

The last time the word *hyper* is used is in verse 37, as part of a compound verb. It says that in all the worst that can happen to us, we are "hyper-conquerors" through the One who loved us (Christ). We are "more than conquerors." We are far more than winners! We may not feel like it, when life comes crashing in on us. We feel like we're just barely surviving. That's why Paul needs to remind us otherwise by putting our suffering into perspective for us. God's love makes us "hyper-conquerors!" We are more than winners! We've got a God who is *hyper*-us, who is on our side! Don't let life's frustration lead you to throw away your victory crown!

Paul says that nothing in all creation can separate us or "put space" between us and the love of God in Christ Jesus our Lord. "If God be for us, who can be against us?" If God loved us so much as to take our place in hell, what further proof do we need that God is absolutely crazy about us? God is for us! God's love has gone "over the top" for us! And no one can drive a wedge between us! So don't *let* anything in your heart stand in the way between you and God. Don't let bitterness over past or present stand in your way. Don't let people stand in your way. Don't let idols stand in your way, anything you love more than God. If you place your faith in Jesus and what he has done for us, nothing can ever come between you and God again.

54

The One and Only Melchizedek Priest

HEBREWS 7:24 REFUTES THE Latter-day Saint claim to have a Melchizedek Priesthood held by millions of priests (that is, every worthy Latter-day Saint male age nineteen and up). When this verse says that Jesus has an "unchangeable priesthood," the word "unchangeable" is actually the Greek *a-parabaton*, which means literally "non-transferable." Jesus is the unique holder of that office. His office cannot be passed to anyone else. He is the one and only Melchizedek priest.

To back that up, let's look at the rest of what the author of Hebrews says about the "order of Melchizedek." The Greek term *taxis* (pronounced "tax-iss") used in this phrase is used only three times in the New Testament outside of this letter, all in the sense of sequential order. The most famous is 1 Corinthians 14:40: "Let all things be done decently and in *order*." In Colossians 2:5, Paul tells the church that he rejoices to see their "order" and the steadfastness of their faith in Christ. In Luke 1:8, Zechariah "executed the priest's office in the *order* of his course." (The NKJV says "in the order of his division," that is, when his unit's turn came to serve on duty).

The references to the "order of Melchizedek" in the book of Hebrews are all based on the Greek translation of Psalm 110:4. Here the word *taxis* is best translated "arrangement" or "classification" (as in our English term "taxonomy," borrowed from this word), because all of the other clues in this letter point to a "classification" or category of priest into which only one member fits. Hebrews 7:11 contrasts the Melchizedek "kind" (*taxis*) of priest with the Aaron "kind" (same word).

Hebrews 7:3 observes that the Melchizedek of Genesis 14 appears to be "made like the Son of God." He appears with no mention of ancestors or descendants. His chief qualifications are that he has "neither a beginning of days nor an end of life," and "remains a priest forever." Some have suggested that this mysterious character is actually a pre-incarnational appearance of Christ himself. While this possibility is attractive, it would require him to be able to bring bread and wine to Abraham, and receive tithes from Abraham, both of which would seem to require a body, which he does not receive until his conception almost two thousand years later. (And Hebrews 9:27 rules out reincarnation.)

Melchizedek is presented in Hebrews as a Lone Ranger, with no established priesthood to which he belongs; Jesus is the same kind of priest. Jesus gets his priesthood, not by DNA or by human decree; he gets it from "the power of an indestructible life" (7:16 NRSV), which is his "likeness" to Melchizedek, whose priesthood continues "forever." We are told that Jesus guarantees a better covenant than the other kind of priests, because they were prevented by death from continuing in office, whereas because Jesus continues forever, he has an "un-transferable" priesthood—it cannot and need not be passed on to anyone else (7:22–24). Because he always lives, Jesus is always able to plead the case of sinners who draw near to God (7:25).

Christ was like Melchizedek in that he got his priesthood straight from God, and passed it on to no one else. I'm sure someone took the original Melchizedek's place at Jerusalem after he was gone, but we have no evidence that there was a Melchizedek "brand" of priest being passed down. Regardless of whether Melchizedek had hands laid on him, or did so for anyone else, the point of Hebrews 7:24 is that Christ's priesthood was unique and non-transferable. Perhaps the only resemblance of Christ's priesthood to Melchizedek's is that he gets it from outside the line of Aaron/Levi, and that it was greater than Levi's, as the writer shows by how Levi's ancestor paid tithes to this mysterious outsider.

So the entire argument in the book of Hebrews is that Jesus' priesthood puts him in a class by himself. No one else is qualified to permanently take away sins. The other kind of priest couldn't do it. Priesthood is all about atonement for sin, not the authority to act for God in any other way. And because of Jesus' once for all sacrifice for sin, there is no longer any need for priesthood of any kind (Hebrews 10:11–18), except the one who always lives to plead our case with God.

The only way that Christians today can speak of priesthood is in a less-than-literal sense. When Christian denominations (such as Catholic, Orthodox, and Episcopal) speak of priests, they are speaking of leaders, pastors, shepherds of souls, not people who atone for sin. And the apostle Peter proclaims what Luther identified as the priesthood of all believers ("you are a royal priesthood," 1 Peter 2:9), a priesthood that includes both women and men, trained and untrained. Because we now have direct access to God (Hebrews 10:19–22), all who trust in the one and only Melchizedek priest for their salvation have authority to speak and act for God, as long as we speak and do only what God has clearly taught in God's word.

So the Bible gives us no evidence for a Melchizedek priesthood with thousands of priests who have authority to speak and act for God. When you as a historic Christian get asked, "Where do you get your authority?", you can say, "From Jesus! You claim you have the Melchizedek priesthood. *I* have the one and only Melchizedek priest!"

55

Words Almost Never Heard in the Bible

> "I hear words I never heard in the Bible!"—Simon and Garfunkel, "Keep the Customer Satisfied," from the album *Bridge Over Troubled Water* (1970)

IT'S SURPRISING HOW MANY words we have thought were in the Bible, until we try to find them: words like retirement, depression, tolerance.

Or, let's start with: "Jesus Loves Me." The Sunday School song says, "This I know, for the Bible tells me so." But just try to find all three words together in such a statement anywhere in the Bible. The closest you'll find is Galatians 2:20 (NRSV), where Paul speaks of his "faith in the Son of God, *who* love*d* me and gave himself for me." The exact words are not there, but the teaching is written in between the lines, all over the New Testament. And yes, it *was* the Christian portion of the Bible that created that belief.

Two famous lines that are often mistaken for Bible quotes are "God helps those who help themselves" (Benjamin Franklin) and "God won't give you more than you can handle." The Bible does contain a close parallel to the latter in 1 Corinthians 10:13, where we are told that God "will not allow you to be tempted above what you are able, but will make with the temptation also a way of escape, so that you may be able to endure it." The exact words are not there, but the idea is there.

"Retirement" is a word worthy of a word study, even though Billy Graham insisted that it was not in his Bible. It *is* in *my* Bible—my Bible says seven times in Numbers 4 that priests were forced to retire after age fifty. (This has implications for how old Zechariah and Elizabeth were when they conceived John the Baptist, because Zechariah was still in the rotation for priestly duty.) Interestingly, Leviticus 27 puts a monetary value on senior citizens that is only half the value of other adults, but the context is paying a vow to God. If you have vowed a senior citizen to God, the amount of money you may give to God in exchange for that person is half of what one would pay for other adults. One could see that as a "senior discount!"

What about the word "depression"? I discovered this puzzle when a group of my college friends who were jokingly dubbed "The Depressed Men" (the name stuck) asked me to translate the name into Hebrew for a tee shirt. It wasn't easy! I tried looking for sadness, but found the generic word "bad" (see chapter 26). Other options are words that could just as easily mean physical pain or sickness (Isaiah 53:3—"a man of *sorrows*, and acquainted with *grief*").

Again, it's not hard to find sadness and depression in the Bible, but it's hard to find a specific word for it there. The best term I can find in Hebrew is the word *yagon*, the opposite of "joy," poetically paired with "sighing," and often translated "sorrow." In Isaiah 35:10 = 51:11 (NRSV), God says the redeemed of the Lord shall return to Zion from exile, and "*sorrow* and sighing shall flee away." Likewise in Jeremiah 31:13, God says, "I will turn their mourning into joy, and I shall comfort them, and I shall make them rejoice from their *sorrow*."

"Depression" is a little easier to find in the Greek Bible, but not by much. The classic noun *athumia* is not found in the New Testament, and only twice in the Septuagint (1 Samuel 1:6, Psalm 119:53), but the verb form (used nine times in the Septuagint) is found in Colossians 3:21, "Parents, do not provoke your children, lest they *become discouraged/depressed*."

Tolerance is touted as such an all-important word today, but where can you find it in the Bible? Jesus says it will be "more tolerable" (*anektoteron*) for Sodom and for Tyre and Sidon on Judgment Day than for the towns who heard him but rejected him (Matthew 10:15 = 11:24 = Luke 10:12). This precise word is used only a total of five times in the Bible, all in the above context. The other times we find the idea in the Bible are extended meanings of words that have a different standard meaning. Psalm 66:18 says, "If I had tolerated (literally "beheld" or "looked upon") sin in my heart, the Lord would not have heard me." And in Revelation 2:20, Jesus criticizes the Thyatira church for being *too* tolerant when he says, "You tolerate (literally "permit") that woman Jezebel," who teaches that fornication and meat offered to idols are OK. Jesus was not as "tolerant" as some imagine!

Where can we find the word "fun" in the Bible? In Proverbs 10:23, we read that doing *zimmah* ("wickedness," which more than half the time means "sex crime") is "sport" to a fool, but wisdom [is sport] to a person of understanding. The word "sport" here is that word that means both "play" and "laughter" (see chapter 24). In 1 Timothy 6:17, we read that God richly gives us all things "for enjoyment" (*apolausis*), a verse that refutes the claim that God is a cosmic killjoy. God actually gives us some wealth for personal enjoyment, as long as it doesn't become an addiction or idolatrous priority.

Hēdonē, the classic word from which we get "hedonism," is found only five times in the New Testament, and thirteen times in the Apocrypha. In Luke 8:14, the sower's good seed is choked out of the human heart by the "pleasures of life." The word has only negative vibes in Titus 3:3, James 4:1 and 4:3, and 2 Peter 2:13. It may be hard to find the word "fun" in the Bible, but we can find pleasure and laughter. We can't find the classic Greek word *eudaimonia* for "happiness" in the Bible, but Jesus does teach us what it means to be "blessed" (*makarios*).

And sorry, cat lovers, but the domestic cat is found nowhere in the Bible except the Epistle of Jeremiah in the Apocrypha, where it says that idols can't be real gods because cats sit on them.

As for the words that Simon and Garfunkel complained they never heard in the Bible, see chapter 4 of this book. Here you'll find words that most pagan Greek authors would never use!

56

How to Do Word Studies for Yourself

THIS BOOK HAS BEEN designed to give you just enough background on the languages of Scripture to make decisions for yourself on how to translate the passages that use the words we have covered in this book, rather than relying exclusively on the Bible translation you're using, or on biblical commentators. Granted, there are countless additional biblical words you may need to know more about as you study God's word. Let's take a look now at how you can do word studies like these yourself, even if you don't know Greek or Hebrew.

Your most handy tool for doing such a word study is an English language concordance. Concordances are most often used to find where and how many times an English word is used in the Bible, especially when one is looking for a specific verse like "To live is Christ, and to die is gain." Look up either the word "live" or "gain," whichever is the least common, and you'll find every Bible verse that uses that word, including the verse you're looking for.

One problem you'll have to work around: the two most popular and easily obtainable concordances are both based on the text of the King James Version. So if you search for a verse based on a wording that is different than the wording in the King James Version, you may not be able to find what you're looking for. So if you look for "the greatest of these is love" by looking up the word "love," you won't find it in either concordance, because the King James Version uses the word "charity" in this verse. Therefore, you need to have a King James Bible handy as the version where you start your word searches, and then try various synonyms to guess how the King James translates the word or verse you're looking for.

The two most popular and easily obtainable Bible concordances are Strong's and Young's (see bibliography). While Strong's is more popular and well-known, I find Young's to be far more user-friendly. Let's take a look at how both concordances work, and then you can make your own decision on which you prefer to use.

Strong's Concordance lists together in one place all uses of a word used in the English Bible. Each verse in which the word is used is marked with a four digit number, which stands for the original Greek or Hebrew word. Look up the number in the dictionary in the back of the concordance, and you'll find the original word, how to pronounce it, and more information about what the word means. Then you can go back to the original listing for your word where you began your search, and locate where else that Greek or Hebrew word for it is used in the Bible. Strong's does not count how many times a word is used; you have to do that yourself.

Young's Concordance lists all uses of an English word in the Bible, and groups them according to each original word. Look up "love," and you'll find three Hebrew words and four Greek words. Look up the Greek or Hebrew word in the back of the concordance, and you'll find other English words that are used to translate the same Greek or Hebrew word. Look up the word for "loving kindness" (spelled *chesed* rather than *ḥesed*, as we transliterate the Hebrew in this book), and you'll find that the word is also translated "kindness" (thirty-eight times), "goodness" (twelve times), and "mercy" (145 times). So you can look up these other English words, and find more verses in which the word *ḥesed* is used.

Let's try an exercise: Where is the verse "A virgin shall conceive"? Look up "virgin." In Strong's concordance, you'll find two Hebrew words (*betulah*—1330, and *ʿalmah*—5959) and one Greek word (*parthenos*—3933). The verse you want is Isaiah 7:14 (quoted in Matthew 1:23). Note that the word is 5959, *ʿalmah*. Some claim that this word means "young woman" and not strictly "virgin." But the Greek Old Testament that Matthew quotes uses the word *parthenos*, which is as specific a word as you can find in Greek for "virgin." Young's concordance tells us that the word can also be found under "damsel" and "maid."

Let's look up *parrēsia* (Strongs's #3954), a word I mentioned back in our Introduction. See how many times the word is translated "boldness," "confidence," or just simply "plainly" or "openly." There is also a verb form, *parrēsiazomai* (Strongs's #3955), often translated "speak boldly/freely." So in Mark 8:32 or Acts 28:31, which meaning of *parrēsia* fits best, in *your* opinion? What do *you* think?

Let's try looking up the word "man." In Strong's Concordance, you'll find *īsh* (#376), *enōsh* (#582), and *adam* (#120) in the Hebrew, and *anthrōpos* (#444) and *anēr/andros* (#435) in the Greek. Now go to Young's Concordance, and we'll see that *īsh* and *anēr/andros* can often mean "husband," but *adam* and *anthrōpos* never do. That's because *adam* and *anthrōpos* can refer to both male and female, and are better translated "human" or "person." In fact, Genesis 1:27 tells us that God made *adam* both "male and female," using the words *zakar* and *neqēbah*, which are as gender-specific as we can get. So when you're reading your Bible, check and see whether "man" is "man (male)" or "person" in the verse you are studying. Numbers 5:6 uses *īsh*, *ishshah* (woman), and *adam* all in the same verse. When the original word is gender-inclusive, why not translate that way?

Once you know the original Greek or Hebrew word you have in mind, you can use advanced biblical commentaries to learn more about the word. If you know how to read Greek or Hebrew writing well enough to look up words, you can use Greek or Hebrew dictionaries. You can also use computer programs which can give you access to these dictionaries, such as the Blue Letter Bible. I happen to use an outdated program called BibleWorks. The company is no longer in business (I bought my copy in 2006), but their product still works just fine for my purposes. BibleWorks has helped me do word searches in the Greek Old Testament, which often helps when a word is used very few times in the New Testament.

Over the past fifty-five chapters, you have seen the basic method I have employed to find the evidence for what a word means and how to assemble that evidence. We look for patterns. We look for synonyms and opposites of the word we are studying. We pay close attention to whatever context we can find. While sometimes I have had to resort to sources that may be unavailable to you, most of my evidence has come from within the Bible itself, and is easily available from a concordance.

It is my hope that you will experience joy in being able to go deeper into God's word by getting to know the actual words God used to communicate that word to those who first heard it!

Bonus Chapter 1

Fun in the Septuagint

THE GREEK VERSION OF the Old Testament, known as the Septuagint, is full of fascinating, surprising, often fun details, most of which you'll never hear about unless you take the time to cruise through the text and find them for yourself. Not everyone is equipped to do so, of course, so I have attempted to package as many of those fun details as I can together here in one place. Even if you're not a language geek like me, I invite you to skim through and glean what you can, and skip the parts that are too technical.

One year I read the entire Hebrew Bible in Hebrew, Greek, and Latin. (I had done this twice for the Pentateuch, but only in Hebrew and Greek. I skimmed the Greek and Latin.) The longer I hang out with the translators who began the Greek Bible project in Egypt around 280 BC, the better I get to know them and how they predictably handle the vocabulary and grammar of God's word.

In the Pentateuch, the Septuagint (known by the symbol LXX) tends to follow the Hebrew Masoretic Text (MT) slavishly. One can account for almost every word, often in the same word order as the Hebrew. When it mistranslates ("proselyte" instead of "sojourner," "power" versus "army," "man man" versus "every man", or its consistently awkward translation of infinitive absolutes), it does so repeatedly. So when the LXX adds, skips, or changes anything, take note! So in Genesis 11, the LXX adds "and he died" for each character on the genealogy. Exodus 1:11 adds to the two store-cities that the Hebrews built "and Ōn, which is Heliopolis." Genesis 46:28 adds "to meet him at Hērōōn, a city in the land of Ramessē."

The LXX often switches "God" and "Lord," which leads to confusion for source critics who base their theory on the use of these names for God to identify sources. It often uses different pronouns than the MT (you or I, versus he). In many cases, the Hebrew text it is translating will switch the Hebrew letters *daleth* and *resh* (Numbers 33:12—*Raphaka* versus *Dophkah*); likewise, "They crossed the crossing" (2 Samuel 19:18) becomes "they labored a labor" in the Greek, reading a *daleth* for a *resh* in the Hebrew manuscript it was translating. Several times in Exodus 25–30 the Greek reads "I will be known" (Nifal form of *ydʿ*) instead of "I will meet by appointment" (Nifal of *yʿd*). Such transposition of letters is common in the LXX, such as in 2 Samuel 7:18, where it reads "you have loved me" (*ʾahabtani*) instead of "you have brought me" (*habiʾotani*, transposing the letter *aleph* to the front of the verb).

The LXX calls Nimrod a *gigas* ("giant," from Greek mythology), as it also calls the Anakim (Deuteronomy 1:28). It calls the Rephaim "Titans" (2 Samuel 5:18). It calls the sea monsters "whales" (Genesis 1:21). It calls discharges *gonorruēs*. It calls Canaan "Phoenicia" once (Exodus 16:35) and the Sidonians "Phoenicians" (Deuteronomy 3:9). It calls the Caphtorim "Cappadocians" (Deuteronomy 2:23). It translates the *Sukkim* of 2 Chronicles 12:3 (a tribe from the western Egyptian desert) as *Troglodytai*, a Sudanese tribe (literally "hole-dwellers"). In Isaiah 23:1, it translates "Wail, O ships of Carthage" for Tyre (see also 23:10). The Septuagint provides much evidence that the Hebrew letter ʿ*ayin* is pronounced like a g: it spells "Gomorrah" for ʿ*Omorrah*, *gomor* for ʿ*omer* (Exodus 16:36), *Raguel* for Reʿ*uel*, *Haggai* for *Ha-ʿAi* (Genesis 13:3), and *Gaibal* for ʿ*Ebal* (Deuteronomy 11:29).

The order of verses and sections of material in the LXX varies wildly in Exodus 35–40. In the Septuagint, Deuteronomy 27:23 adds "Cursed be whomever lies with his wife's sister." The LXX adds details on Nahash the Ammonite in 1 Samuel 11, while it shortens the account of David and Goliath, it drops the reference to Eli's sons sleeping with the women who served at the sanctuary in 1 Samuel 2:22, and it shortens Jeremiah by 12% and drastically reorders its contents. In Numbers 24:7, the Septuagint reads "Gog" for "Agag." And in Esther 8:17, when the Persian king comes out in defense of the Jews, many of the pagans not only "Judaized" (same word as Paul uses in Galatians 2:14), but also "circumcised themselves" (*not* in the Hebrew text).

Out of twenty-eight times that the term *Amen* occurs in the Hebrew Bible, the Septuagint translates it twenty-three times with the word *genoito* ("let it happen"). It uses *exstasis* for the *tardemah* or "deep sleep" that God puts on Adam before creating Eve (Genesis 2:21). In Genesis 21:22 and 21:32, the Septuagint calls Phicol the king's *nymphagogos* or "leader of the bride." It calls the lords (*seranim*) of the Philistines *satrapes*, a much later Persian term (1 Samuel 5:8). In Numbers 11:20, Israel shall eat quail "until it becomes *cholera* for you." The name *Elisheba* becomes "Elizabeth" in Exodus 6:23. And although *erōs* and its related verb *eraō* are found nowhere in the New Testament, the two are found a total of five times in the Septuagint, including Esther 2:17 ("The king loved Esther"), Proverbs 4:6 ("Love wisdom"), Proverbs 7:18 ("let's delight ourselves with *erōs*"), and Proverbs 30:16, where the Greek mistakenly reads "the *erōs* of a woman" rather than "the barren womb." In addition, the noun *erastēs* (lover) occurs a total of fourteen times: Jeremiah 4:30, 22:20, and 22:22, Lamentations 1:19, Ezekiel 16:33, 16:36–37, 23:5, 23:9, and 23:22, and Hosea 2:7, 9, 12, 14, and 15.

The LXX uses the optative mood (a verb form used for wishes and hypothetical statements) more than five hundred times (versus sixty-seven times for the New Testament); Job is particularly chock-full of optatives. The LXX often uses *edomai* instead of *phagomai* as the future of *esthiō*, "I eat." In Exodus 32:26, it uses the rare form *itō* as a future imperative of *erchomai*, "I come" (also used in a variant reading in John 7:34).

While the LXX Pentateuch transliterates beer as *sikēra*, 1 Samuel translates it very literally as *methusma* ("that which makes drunk"). In Song of Solomon, it translates "love" (*dodīm*) as "breasts," and "female companion" (*rēʿah*) as *plēsion* ("neighbor"). In Isaiah 24:20, the Septuagint uses the Greek verb "to have a hangover" (*kraipalaō*). It often uses *tharsei* ("take courage") for *ʾal-tiyra* ("Do not fear"—Exodus 20:20), and it sometimes uses *eusebeia* for the fear of the Lord (Isaiah 11:2). It translates *drakōn* for *tannīn* in Exodus 7:9, "donkey-centaur" for "satyr" (Isaiah 34:14), "sirens" for "jackals" (Isaiah 34:13, 43:20), and "dung" on the ground becomes a *paradigma* ("pattern/example/lesson") on the ground in Jeremiah 8:2. And three times (including Esther 2:3 and 2:9) it uses the word *smēgma*, although in the Septuagint it refers to a facial beauty treatment, as opposed to what the word means in English (Red Dwarf fans know what I'm talking about!).

The Septuagint has hundreds of Greek words that occur nowhere else in Greek literature. They are usually not Egyptian dialectical words, but simply compound words that are easy enough to understand, but that no other Greek writer ever uses.

One more fun surprise in the Septuagint: in the kosher food lists, we find two unexpected creatures: an insect called the "snake-fighter" (Leviticus 11:22), and the giraffe (Deuteronomy 14:5). Who knew these were kosher? For more on these two fun details, I refer you to my article "Kosher in the Greek?" (see bibliography, or find the link at www.biblicalethic.org).

Bonus Chapter 2

Fun in the Latin Bible

The Latin Bible is full of surprising, sometimes peculiar, sometimes humorous fun details to explore. Here in this chapter, I will package as many of them together as possible, for the benefit of those who have never had time to find them, and/or for those who have never had Latin. If you haven't, never fear—no advance knowledge of Latin needed.

Hanging out with Saint Jerome in his Latin version of the Bible has given me the chance to get to know him, as I watch how he renders the original text. I find that he often translates the Hebrew Bible more accurately than the Greek translators of 280 BC (who were Jewish), possibly because he learned his Hebrew in Bethlehem rather than in Egypt. I also see that his version bears witness to a Hebrew text that is closer to the Masoretic or standard Hebrew text than the Hebrew original on which the Greek version is based. Jerome's version gives us a glimpse of what a proto-Masoretic text looked like in AD 400. I truly appreciate what Jerome and those who preceded him have given us!

In an age where large numbers of Latin-speaking Christians had their own private translation of the New Testament, with all sorts of variations of spelling, grammar, vocabulary, and textual originals, Jerome deserves a lot of credit for wading through the multiplicity of Old Latin texts and creating one standard version. One example would be where the angel urges Joseph to take Mary as his wife. Some Old Latin copies read *uxorem*, the standard word for "wife," but some manuscripts say *coniugem*, "mate," someone with whom one "mates" or "conjugates," a word that implies a sexual relationship. Those translators who used the term *uxorem* seem to reject any notion of such a relationship between Joseph and Mary, even after Jesus is born. For his Vulgate, Jerome chose *coniugem*.

Jerome often puts explanatory notes that are not in the original Hebrew, straight into the text. In Deuteronomy 23:2, he quotes the Hebrew term *mamzer* (illegitimate child) by simply transliterating it, and then adding *hoc est, de scortō natus* ("that is, one who is born from a harlot"). In Joshua 3:16, he says that the waters of the Jordan drained away into *mare Solitudinis, quod nunc vocātur Mortuum* ("the Sea of the Desert, which is now called [Sea] of the Dead"). He explains the name Kiriath-Jearim in Joshua 15:9 by adding *id est urbs silvārum*, "that is, City of Forests." He identifies Ararat as "Armenia" (Genesis 8:4). And nineteen times he uses the Latin calendar term *kalendae* ("first of the month") for "new moon."

Jerome almost never uses the noun *amor* or the verb *amāre* to refer to either the love of God (three times) or love between believers (zero times); the noun he uses is *caritas* (from which we get "charity" in 1 Corinthians 13), and the verb he consistently uses is *dīligere*.

Jerome also uses the noun *uterus* in ways that are typical of Latin but are foreign to our ears. In Genesis 15:4, God speaks to Abraham of an heir who will be born *de uterō tuō*, "from your (Abraham's!) *uterus*" (presumably meaning "body"). Likewise, David refers in 2 Samuel 16:11 to the son who came forth *de uterō meō*, "from my body." The most surprising example is Jonah praying *de uterō piscis*, "from the belly of the fish" (Jonah 2:1). And in a large number of texts where we find the English term "womb," we find the Latin word *vulva* rather than *uterus* (usually as the object of the verb "to open"); the two Latin words are even paired as synonyms in Job 3:11, Psalm 58:3, Isaiah 46:3, and Jeremiah 1:5.

It is the Latin version that specifies whether the *aetos* that is crying woe on the earth in Revelation 8:13 is an eagle or a vulture (like the Hebrew *nesher*, *aetos* can mean either); the Latin tradition (whether it is correct, who knows?) says *aquila*, which can only mean "eagle", not a *vultur*. The Latin identifies the almug wood of 1 Kings 10:11–12 as thyine or citron wood, the most expensive wood of Roman times. And the Latin tells us in 1 Kings 15:13 that Asa removed Maacah from being queen mother because she had made a most obscene (*turpissimum*) image of Priapus. (Mom! How disgusting can you get?)

The Latin also adds punch to the evils spoken of in Job 31:11 (lusting for a virgin, or for someone's wife) and Leviticus 20:13 (same-sex intercourse) as being not just *malum* (bad), but *nefas* (a notorious evil), the same word used by the people when Saul decreed that Jonathan should die (*hoc nefas est!*—1 Samuel 14:45). And the evil demanded by the men of Gibeah is called *scelus hoc contra naturam* (Judges 19:24—the words "contrary to nature" are added by Jerome to the text).

The heretic Marcion's famous refrain of denial, *Absit!* ("Far be it!", as quoted many times by Tertullian) is used thirty-two times in the Latin Bible. Abraham says to God in Genesis 18:25, *Absit a tē* ("Far be it from thee") to slay the righteous with the wicked! The people say to Joshua in Joshua 24:16, *Absit a nobīs* ("Far be it from us") to forsake the Lord. And *Absit!* becomes the standard way to translate Paul's famous line, *Mē genoito!* ("May it never be!"), while the Hebrew *amen* is rendered, *Fiat!*

Sometimes, the Latin goes beyond the meaning of the original; while Jacob complains in Genesis 31:42 that Laban almost sent him away "empty" (*rēqam*), the Latin has him say *nudum* ("naked"!). In Esther 5:14, 8:7 and 9:25, a seventy-five-foot gallows is called a *crux* (cross). Sometimes, there is even confusion: in Judges 15:19, where the Hebrew says that God opened the *maktesh* (ground-down or "hollow [place]") at Lehi, and water came forth, the Latin says that God opened the molar tooth (another meaning of *maktesh*) in the jawbone (the meaning of the place-name Lehi) of the *donkey* (not in the text at all in this verse!), and water came forth (!). In 1 Samuel 15:4, where Saul numbers his troops "in Telaim," the Latin reads *quasi agnōs*, "as if they were lambs."

But sometimes the Latin is more literal than our Bibles. While the Hebrew of Judges 3:24 says that Eglon must be "covering his feet," the Latin says *purgat alvum* ("he is emptying his bowel"—similarly, 1 Samuel 24:4). When the men of Gibeah demand that the Levite be brought out to them "so that we may know him" (Judges 19:22), the Greek says literally "know him," but the Latin reads "so that we may abuse (*abutāmur*) him." In Genesis 43:34, while our Bibles say that Joseph's brothers "were merry" with him, both the Latin, the Greek, and the Hebrew say that they "got drunk" with him (Hebrew *wayyishkeru*, Greek *emethysthēsan*, Latin *inebriatī sunt*). Here is one example of why we must not take a "monkey-see, monkey-do" approach to the behavior of biblical characters, but must rely on clear ethical teaching passages such as Ephesians 5:18 in a case like this.

The Latin Bible is a wonderful supplement to textbooks such as Wheelock for those who are first learning Latin. There are copious examples of future active and passive participles, all four subjunctives, and both positive and negative question markers. Sarah asks in Genesis 18:13, *Num vērē paritura sum, anus?* ("Am I, an old lady, really about to give birth?") *Num*, a word used fifty-four times in the Vulgate, signals that she expects a "No" answer. Cain clearly implies a "No" answer when he asks in Genesis 4:9, *Num custos fratris mei sum?* The Latin Bible also regularly uses forms that Wheelock told us were rare, such as *īvit* for "he has gone" (twenty times), the plural of *inquit* (*inquiunt*, "they said," used seven times), and *estō* for "let it be" (eighty-two times in the singular, sixty times in the plural *estōte*).

We are so thankful that somebody translated God's word into the language of the Roman Empire, a resource destined to have a huge impact on the world for centuries. For Protestants like myself, the Vulgate carries no authority in itself as a version compared to others. Like the King James Version, it is merely a fascinating witness at one point in time to the text of God's word that it translates, and it gives us clues to how that text was understood and was communicated to the *vulgus* (common people) who were that version's intended audience.

Select Bibliography

Alinsky, Saul D. *Rules for Radicals*. New York: Random House, 1971.
Bailey, Kenneth. "The Manger and the Inn: A Middle-Eastern View of the Birth Story of Jesus." *Presbyterian Outlook*, Dec 21, 2006. https://pres-outlook.org/2006/12/the-manger-and-the-inn-a-middle-eastern-view-of-the-birth-story-of-jesus/.
Bauer, Walter, Frederick W. Danker, W. F. Arndt, and F. W. Gingrich. *A Greek-English Lexicon of the New Testament and Other Early Christian Literature*. 3rd ed. Chicago: University of Chicago Press, 2000.
Clement of Alexandria. *Christ the Educator*. Volume 23 in *The Fathers of the Church*, edited by Roy Joseph Deferrari et al. Translated by Simon P. Wood. Washington, D.C.: Catholic University of America Press, 1953.
Danby, Herbert. *The Mishnah: Translated from the Hebrew with Introduction and Brief Explanatory Notes*. Oxford: Oxford University Press, 1933.
Gordon, C. H., ed. *Ugaritic Textbook*. 3 vols. Analecta Orientalia 38. Rome: Pontifical Biblical Institute, 1965.
Gordon, Cyrus. "'*Almah* in Isaiah 7:14." *Journal of Bible and Religion* 21.2 (1953) 240–41.
Hobson, G. Thomas. "*Aselgeia* in Mark 7:22." *Filologia Neotestamentaria* 21 (2008) 65–74.
———. "Cut Off From (One's) People." PhD diss., Concordia Seminary St. Louis, 2010.
———. "Kosher in the Greek: The Giraffe and the Snake-Fighter?" *Zeitschrift für Altorientalische und Biblische Rechtsgeschichte* 19 (2014) 307–12.
Hobson, Tom. *What's on God's Sin List for Today?* Eugene, OR: Wipf and Stock, 2011.
Houten, Christiana van. *The Alien in Israelite Law: A Study of the Changing Legal Status of Strangers in Ancient Israel*. Sheffield: Journal for the Study of the Old Testament, 1991.
Hultin, Jeremy F. *The Ethics of Obscene Speech in Early Christianity and Its Environment*. Leiden: Brill, 2008.
Kitchen, K. A. *On the Reliability of the Old Testament*. Grand Rapids: Eerdmans, 2003.
Koehler, Ludwig, and Walter Baumgartner. *Hebrew and Aramaic Lexicon of the Old Testament*. 2 vols. Revised study edition. Translated by M. E. J. Richardson. Leiden: Brill, 2001.
Krantz, Judith. "Living Together Is a Rotten Idea." *Cosmopolitan* 181.4 (Oct 1976) 218–27.
Liddell, Henry George, Robert Scott, and Henry Stuart Jones. *A Greek-English Lexicon*. 9th ed. Oxford: Clarendon, 1996.

Lundström, Steven. "The Hunt Is on Again! Tiglath-pileser I's and Aššur-bel-kala's nāḫirū-Sculptures in Assur." In *Stories of Long Ago: Festschrift für Michael Roaf*, edited by H. D. Baker et al., 323–38. Alter Orient und Altes Testament 397. Münster: Ugarit Verlag, 2012.

Meier, John P. *A Marginal Jew: Rethinking the Historical Jesus*. 5 vols. New York: Doubleday, 2001–.

Price, James. "Rosh: An Ancient Land Known to Ezekiel." *Grace Theological Journal* 6.1 (1985) 67–89.

Rushdoony, Rousas John. *Institutes of Biblical Law*. 3 vols. Nutley: Craig, 1973.

Ruthven, Jon Marc. *The Prophecy That Is Shaping History*. Fairfax: Xulon, 2003.

Spicq, Ceslas. *Theological Lexicon of the New Testament*. 3 vols. Translated by James D. Ernest. Peabody, MA: Hendrickson, 1994.

Strong, James. *The Exhaustive Concordance of the Bible*. Nashville: Abingdon, 1977.

Walton, John. "The Antediluvian Section of the Sumerian King List and Genesis 5." *Biblical Archaeologist* 44.4 (1981) 207–8.

———. *The Lost World of Genesis One: Ancient Cosmology and the Origins Debate*. Downers Grove: IVP Academic, 2009.

Wesley, John. *A Plain Account of Christian Perfection*. Kansas City: Beacon Hill, 1958.

Young, Robert. *Young's Analytical Concordance to the Bible*. Nashville: Thomas Nelson, 1980.

Younker, Randall W., and Richard M. Davidson. "The Myth of the Solid Heavenly Dome." In *The Genesis Account and Its Reverberations in the Old Testament*, edited by Gerald A. Klingbell, 31–56. Berrien Springs: Andrews University Press, 2015.

www.ingramcontent.com/pod-product-compliance
Lightning Source LLC
Chambersburg PA
CBHW062043220426

43662CB00010B/1630